Planting Nature

Planting Nature

TREES AND THE MANIPULATION
OF ENVIRONMENTAL STEWARDSHIP
IN AMERICA

SHAUL E. COHEN

UNIVERSITY OF CALIFORNIA PRESS
Berkeley   Los Angeles   London

University of California Press
Berkeley and Los Angeles, California

University of California Press, Ltd.
London, England

Library of Congress Cataloging-in-Publication Data

Cohen, Shaul Ephraim, 1961–.
   Planting nature : trees and the manipulation of environmental stew-
ardship in America / Shaul E. Cohen.
       p.   cm.
   Includes bibliographical references and index.
   ISBN 0-520-23770-6 (cloth: alk. paper).
   1. Afforestation—United States.   2. Afforestation—Environmental
aspects—United States.   3. Afforestation—Government policy—
United States.   I. Title.

SD409.C5495   2004
333.75'152'0973—dc22   2003019073

Manufactured in Canada

13   12   11   10   09   08   07   06   05   04
10   9   8   7   6   5   4   3   2   1

For my parents, Joshua and Lisa

It can also happen, if will and grace are joined, that as I contemplate the tree I am drawn into a relation, and the tree ceases to be an It.

The tree is no impression, no play of my imagination, no aspect of a mood; it confronts me bodily and has to deal with me as I must deal with it—only differently.

Martin Buber, *I and Thou*, 1937

Contents

Acknowledgments

This book has been quite some time in the making. Most of it has been a pleasure to do, in large part because of the people that I have worked with along the way. In many respects the acknowledgments section is my favorite part; it serves as a record of the many good experiences I have had. To begin, then, I thank many people at the University of Oregon. A number of students have been part of this project, among them Lisa Mody, Kristen Schulyer, and Tony Leiserowitz. Two students in particular, Annie Hommel and Tara Corbett, made enormous contributions and cheerfully waded in where I refused to go. The enthusiasm of my students has buoyed me all along the way. I am also grateful to my comrades in the Department of Geography—Alec Murphy, Andrew Marcus, Bart Bartlein, Cathy Whitlock, Jim Meachem, Lise Nelson, Pat McDowell, Peter Walker, Ron Wixman, and Susan Hardwick, especially those members of the Human Geography Writer's Group who slogged through this book with me chapter by chapter. My work is far better for their time, energy, and dedication. Two other colleagues here, Matthew Dennis and

David Frank, have been unstinting in their help and unflinching in their challenges to my writing. I have not done quite as well as they wanted perhaps, but I have tried to justify their effort on my behalf. Vickie Staffelbach and Mary Milo have worked hard and with good spirit to keep me out of bureaucratic purgatory; my thanks to them as well. I have received financial support from the university's Humanities Center and the Center for the Study of Women in Society through a Rockefeller-funded program, "Ecological Conversations," and I am grateful to those affiliated with them for making that possible.

I received additional financial support from the Newbury Library in Chicago and the Forest History Society in Durham, North Carolina. I apologize to the Forest History Society for arriving along with an epic hurricane on my first visit and a record snowfall on my second. It was, despite it all, a pleasure to work there. Anyone interested in doing research on forestry and forest history in the United States will be well served by connecting with Cheryl Oakes, the librarian of the Forest History Society, who is a wonderful hub of information and communication networks in the scholarly community. I am also grateful to John Rosenow and the staff of the National Arbor Day Foundation, Deborah Gangloff and the staff of American Forests, Derek Jumper at the American Forest and Paper Association, and many people at other organizations and agencies. Wherever I have gone, people have been eager to talk about trees and their work and to share their time and stories. Steve Cafferata, a Weyerhaeuser tree planter and forest economist, has been a kind teacher to me, and I have enjoyed our conversations and trips in the field very much. I have also benefited from the support of Stan Holwitz, Dore Brown, and Bonita Hurd, who have done a great job for me at the University of California Press. Barbara and Lou Ravitz have always provided a warm home away from home.

Some other people in Eugene deserve special mention. Carl Johannessen made his land available, and, side by side, we planted and cared for an awful lot of trees, hoping all the while that they would get big and outlive us both by a long way. Dennis Lueck, specifically of the Eugene Tree Foundation and more generally of Eugene as a whole, is my own tree hero and the best example I know of a true steward. Sarah, Sam,

Raya, Talia, Sammy, Leah, Leora, and their parents have kept me moving joyfully from season to season.

Even closer to home, I owe special mention to a number of individuals. First, I owe a debt to the dawn redwood planted in my front lawn about the time I began researching this book. It has been growing like gangbusters since then and given me pleasure daily. Though my neighbors think it is a bit odd that I spend so much time with it, they too have grown attached to its progress and invested in its health. Blake, Kelly, and Eliav have also done a lot of growing during the same period, and this has been a wonder to behold too. Eliav has helped me plant a lot of trees, and his enthusiasm for their future has been a source of delight. I also thank my wife and best friend, Diane Baxter. She has helped me with all I have written, supported my work and shared her work with me, and endured or indulged all my enthusiasms in a wonderful way. She has sacrificed a lot on my behalf and on behalf of this book, and I am forever grateful. Finally, I am beholden to the trees, each one a special part of nature.

ONE Taking Control of Nature

> When we consider the immense collateral advantages
> derived from the presence of the forest, the terrible evils
> necessarily resulting from its destruction, we can not but
> admit that the preservation of existing woods, and the
> more costly extension and creation of them where they
> have been unduly reduced or have never existed, are
> among the plainest dictates of self-interest and most
> obvious of the duties which this age owes to those that
> are to come after it.
>
> George Perkins Marsh, 1863

Trees have a particular and powerful hold on American conceptions of what is good in nature and the environment. As we attempt to cope with environmental crises, we increasingly enlist trees as agents of our stewardship over nature. Trees have long been invested with positive associations and symbols; they are powerful mechanisms for carrying out different agendas because their meanings and uses can be manipulated and directed to a variety of ends. Together with their utilitarian value, this symbolic power casts them as prominent actors on the human stage. In this book, I examine the phenomenon of deputizing trees to do our environmental bidding, a subject I find troubling in a number of ways.

My concern stems at least in part from my broader curiosity about human conduct in the face of unfolding environmental problems. How and why do people maintain such seeming disregard for the need to

1

transform the way we operate in our world, and for the need to change our fundamental orientation toward nature? Moreover, I am drawn to the paradoxical behavior of those who seem (and say that they are) committed to stewardship of the environment and yet make no serious effort to truly protect it. If those who profess devotion to nature are part of the problem, rather than part of the solution, how do they maintain their self-image as environmental stewards? Ultimately, I ask what interests are served by certain practices we consider pro-environmental, and how do those with power maintain their interests even as we learn more and more about the damage being done to our world?

I argue that trees serve as a bridge that helps connect disparate interest groups in the struggle to set the environmental agenda. That link, however, does not increase our ability to work toward a more harmonious relationship with nature. Rather, it undermines it. It is not that trees are harmful to the environment, but that an adoration of trees creates what is at best a double-edged sword wielded not only by environmentalists but also by their antagonists. The writer Michael Pollan suggests that our "thoughts and metaphors cling" to trees "like iron filings to a magnet. Obviously trees exist apart from our evolving pictures of them— we didn't invent them—but trees were married to our metaphors so long ago, we have no idea what they would look like single."[1] The very power of trees, our love of them, and their prevalence in our cultural works and iconography make the manipulation of trees and, more important, of the idea of what trees can do, extremely problematic.

To illustrate my argument, I examine the hoopla around tree planting in the post–Earth Day era, particularly in the last fifteen years or so. Three sectors have sponsored or carried out the bulk of tree planting in the United States: the timber industry, the government, and the nonprofit citizens groups that advocate conservation of the environment.[2] In terms of sheer numbers of trees, the timber industry plants the most, followed by the government, and then by membership or sponsored organizations open to the public. The timber companies and their affiliated professional associations speak loudly and regularly about their tree planting, promoting the many benefits for society and the environment said to accrue from their work. The government is, of course, eager to advertise its tree planting programs, whether they operate at the neighborhood or national level. I examine the timber industry and government sectors but highlight the nonprofit groups by offering a more focused analysis of them, because I feel the citizens groups that seek to enlist public support for and participation in tree planting activities play a critical role. It is there, where "average" people interact with the environment through tree planting (in whatever intimate or distant way a particular program allows), that a bond is forged between the individual who plants a single tree and those who plant many more trees—the government and industrial planters. The bond stems from the sense of common cause articulated and facilitated by actors in each of the planting sectors, in both direct and indirect ways. Though this has positive practical consequences on a small scale, it leads to troubling political, economic, cultural, and environmental consequences on a far greater scale. The common cause articulated by the tree planting discourse suggests that everyone profits from tree planting; in fact, what we all share, often unequally, is the cost of environmental degradation. Profit may come in small measure to those who plant trees, but the lion's share is reserved for capital interests that give us notions of Eden-on-earth, though in this case it is a man-made rather than a divine affair.[3]

THE PROTAGONISTS

Two popular groups lie at the center of my inquiry into nongovernmental organizations, and they may be familiar to many people. The American Forests association and the National Arbor Day Foundation are leaders in the nonprofit tree planting sector. American Forests bills itself as the oldest conservation organization in the country. Its history is marked by continuing organizational weakness and a changing sense of mission, but also by a steadfast advocacy on behalf of the forests of the United States. Formed in 1875 as the American Forestry Association, American Forests has had a close though not always congenial relationship with captains of the timber industry, as well as with small woodlot owners throughout the country, and in the past it has often had strong bonds with the U.S. Forest Service. In recent years, American Forests has sought to position itself a bit more as an environmental organization, in addition to being a conservation organization, primarily via its Global ReLeaf tree planting program.

The National Arbor Day Foundation is a much younger organization, begun in 1972 to mark the centennial of Arbor Day, which was created by the Nebraska politician and tree lover J. Sterling Morton. The National Arbor Day Foundation is less overtly political in its work, but the utilitarian current that runs through both Arbor Day and the foundation certainly serves political ends. The foundation reaches a broader audience than American Forests, primarily because of its connection to Arbor Day—which is part of the curriculum in most American schools—and its direct mail and other advertising campaigns. After purchasing a ten-dollar annual membership, individuals receive ten trees in the mail at no additional charge, or the donation supports the preservation of tropical rain forests via one of the foundation's programs. In many respects, the National Arbor Day Foundation is a darling of the American establishment, as it provides a safe haven for conservation action, removed from the polarizing environmental debates that often swirl around trees and forests. Its overly simple yet powerful advertisements in print, radio, and video circulate both as free public service announcements and as paid ads sponsored by the government trumpeting Morton's basic charge: "Plant Trees."

Government sponsorship of tree planting is straightforward when it comes to promoting National Arbor Day Foundation advertisements, but far more involved when it supports the work of nonprofit tree planting groups, civic organizations, local governments, woodlot owners, and the timber industry. In an ongoing transition, the federal government is shifting from primarily being a tree planter—on the cutover lands of the national forests—to being a tree-planting facilitator who supports or subsidizes planting by others on a range of public and private nonfederal lands, as well as in the national forests and other areas. It provides this support through programs operated by the Forest Service and other agencies.

The timber industry—the largest tree planter in the United States—

produces nearly 1 billion seedlings annually.[4] While planting trees is in its economic interests (insuring that there will be a crop to harvest in the future), the industry did not always have such long-range vision. Michael Williams has chronicled the deforestation of the United States as a process that moved from east to west across the continent with the advance of settlement and industry.[5] Only when the finite nature of the standing timber became undeniable did the timber industry as a whole turn to tree planting to extend its own existence and to comply with increasing government regulation (see fig. 1).[6] Just as the industry came to appreciate the need to plant trees, so too has it come to realize the importance of being seen as helpful to the environment. It proudly boasts that it plants more trees than anyone else, thus qualifying as the environmental steward par excellence.

This bold claim for recognition as an environmentally beneficial industry is proffered by many individual timber companies and by trade associations as well, foremost among them the American Forest and Paper Association, through its trademarked Sustainable Forestry Initiative. The association provides guidelines for accreditation through the initiative and draws attention to its voluntary efforts to improve forestry practices. Yet while the initiative may improve forest practices, the effort seems designed to preempt outside monitoring and—worse yet from the industry's perspective—interference in timber company policies. The ongoing controversies over deforestation globally, the loss of old-growth forests in the Pacific Northwest, and the conflicts over clear-cutting elsewhere in the United States all clearly influence an industry that has, at least since the mid–twentieth century, been conscious of public perceptions and how they may affect profits.

One additional sector involved in tree planting for profit is the non-timber-related commercial world. As environmentalism has gained cachet, businesses have learned that giving themselves a "green" image is good marketing.[7] As a result, an enormous array of manufacturers and service providers have initiated or subscribed to some form of tree planting program. The spectrum is as broad as the economy itself: sponsors include car manufacturers, steel foundries, software makers, communications companies, retail chains, and oil companies. Figure 2 shows

Isn't it about time for us to plant the trees for our great, great, etc. grandson's bungalow since we are cutting down our timber each year six times as fast as it can grow and it takes 300 years to grow a good sawlog? (1921)

Figure 1. In 1921, popular culture already reflected some skepticism about claims that tree planting sufficiently compensated for timber harvesting. Cartoon by Jay N. "Ding" Darling, 1921.

Figure 2. This decorated oil storage tank stands in Eugene, Oregon. Photo by author.

a scene painted on an oil storage tank in Eugene, Oregon, that depicts a forest with old trees, harvested timber, and reforestation, graphically illustrating a way that industry can dress itself in an image of trees and forest. One of my favorite advertisements appeared in the *New York Times* in 1997. It promotes Tommy Hilfiger's Tommy Girl perfume by linking it with the upcoming Earth Day. The hook is trees. Consumers are offered *"a free plantable fir tree sapling* [provided by American Forests] just for the pleasure of your company."[8] The promotion then taps into the impending Mother's Day and encourages the purchase of a Tommy Hilfiger product to "show her your love is evergreen!" To the business world, it is clear that trees are both versatile and profitable.

WHY TREES?

To explain at least in part why trees are so popular and make such a powerful vehicle requires a brief look in two different directions: at the deep cultural underpinnings that invest trees with meaning, and at the current utilitarian value ascribed to trees. I am interested primarily in the tree imagery of Western civilizations, though trees are a common cultural currency throughout the world. In the United States, the foundation stories of creation that come from the Middle East place trees at the center. The textual roots of Judaism, Christianity, and Islam grow from the Garden of Eden, of course, home to perhaps the most famous tree of all, the Tree of Life (Genesis chapters 2 and 3). Much has been made of this tree, an emblem of a web of associations between trees (many of which could live longer than humans, particularly before inventions such as modern medicine and the chainsaw) and immortality.

Certainly monotheisms have no monopoly on the veneration of trees, and the meanings, symbols, and deification of trees in animist cultures (and monotheist cultures, as noted by Simon Schama) have been plotted out by scholars such as Sir James Frazer in *The Golden Bough* and Mircea Eliade in *Patterns in Comparative Religion*.[9] According to Eliade, "We meet sacred trees . . . in the history of every religion, in popular tradition the world over, in primitive metaphysics and mysticism, to say nothing of iconography and popular art."[10] Robert Graves explores the link between trees, myth, and the Celtic alphabet (the name of each letter being a different tree) in *The White Goddess*, showing how intimately culture and trees can be intertwined. According to Graves, the study of early European (and some Mediterranean) mythology "is based squarely on tree-lore and seasonal observation of life in the fields."[11]

In the similarly influenced but deistically more constrained Bible, the tree serves as a referent to the human, as an individual and as a nation (Israel). Thus whatever may be sacred in the tree is not left as an external manifestation of holiness, but rather is internalized as a reflection of woman and man. The first Psalm (1:1–3) suggests, "Happy is the man . . . who delights in the law of the Lord / And he shall be like a tree planted by streams of water / That brings forth its fruit in its season / And whose leaf does not wither." And Psalm 92:12–13 states, "The righteous shall blossom like the palm tree / He shall grow like a cedar in Lebanon. Planted in the house of the Lord / They shall blossom in God's Courtyard." In addition to offering vivid metaphorical imagery of the trees, the Bible and associated texts deal with trees as economic or sustenance items and lay out a range of laws that protect trees from human depredation. The biblical admonition that fruit trees could not be cut down to promote a siege in war reflects the sacrificing of trees for human needs. Use was not always destructive or negative of course, and there were laws that gave the poor access to fruit trees and that regulated use and ownership of the trees. Whether dealing with the positive utilitarian aspects of trees or their protection, the Bible offers a link to humans, pointedly observing in the book of Isaiah (65:22), "For as the days of the tree shall be the days of My people." The place of trees in the Bible and the books of the Prophets was noted by the environmentalist Aldo Leopold, who observes that "Isaiah was the [Teddy] Roosevelt of the Holy Land," and that Joel was "the preacher of conservation of watersheds."[12] Leopold goes on to praise the silvicultural skills of a number of biblical figures and notes the keen awareness of the natural world expressed in the stories they tell as they describe their use of the land.

The early linkage between people and trees, intended to protect the latter from the former, presages an inherent tension between a utilitarian orientation and the constant association of trees with symbol and meaning. Many historians believe that the story of wood, or perhaps the chronicle of deforestation, is the story of civilization itself.[13] In early stories, there is also a parochialization of trees in terms of different species or types of tree: distinct forests are associated with particular human groups and the rise and fall of their fortunes.

Within this school of thought about the story of civilization, a particular track follows the fortunes of empires in relation to the availability of a sufficient supply of wood. According to J. V. Thirgood, John Perlin, and others, empires, such as those of the Romans and Greeks, expanded in search of additional wood, having consumed their domestic supply in the course of economic growth. As they pursued wood (and other materials) at increasingly great distances, their supply lines became overextended and, thereby, weakened, and the empires went into decline. Whether or not one chooses to organize history along such lines, it is clear that some in these empires grew concerned about their wood supply, the environmental degradation that came with deforestation, and the need to undertake some effort toward remediation.

Clarence J. Glacken's *Traces on the Rhodian Shore* yields an illustration of this early environmental concern and shows that an awareness of trees as a critical feature of the environment is not new.[14] Glacken describes, among many examples, Ptolemaic tree planting in Egypt during the third century B.C.E. to produce food, create parks, and protect waterways. Richard Grove notes the Venetian call to reforest land along watercourses in order to slow the silt flowing into the Venice Lagoon in the 1450s.[15] By the early nineteenth century, Grove argues, tree planting had come to be "seen as [an] essential component of radical social reform and political reconstruction" in the islands of British colonization.[16]

That attitude has its roots in the work of Sir John Evelyn, often called the father of scientific forestry. Evelyn was commissioned by the British Royal Society to do a study of the timber crisis in seventeenth-century Great Britain. Apprehending that the fate of the empire rested on a sufficient supply of timber for shipbuilding, and particularly for making tall masts, the society charged Evelyn with taking stock of the timber reserves in Britain and charting a course for their conservation. He took an aggressive approach to planting, and this is reflected in the full title of his 1664 report, *Sylva, or a Discourse on Forest-Trees, and the Propagation of Timber in His Majesties [sic] Dominions.*[17]

Evelyn's call for tree planting was endorsed by the Crown and taken up by Britain's aristocracy in part because Evelyn married patriotism (and support of the king) with reforestation. The English gentry held tree planting competitions in the mid– and late eighteenth century, and Schama presents Colonel Thomas Johnes of Cardiganshire as the most industrious of all; "between 1795 and 1801 [he] planted over two million trees, and raised, according to his claim, 922,000 oaks."[18] Evelyn himself bragged of *Sylva* being the inspiration for the planting of 2 million trees (later reduced by modesty to 1 million). The link between tree planting, patriotism, and power was found in other European maritime states as well, and was later propagated in the American colonies.

WHAT DO TREES DO?

Whether in biblical Israel, ancient Rome, medieval Venice, or Elizabethan England, trees were tapped both to provide something physical—a resource or environmental tool—and to build moral fiber and civic values. That same duality holds today. Though trees may no longer be objects of worship in mainstream Western cultures, they are still venerated in both tangible and metaphorical ways.

The timber industry, the government, and nonprofit groups are all eager to promote the many uses of trees and the special benefits of planting them. They proffer long lists of benefits for the individual (e.g., promoting emotional stability), the community (an enhanced sense of citizenship in children), and the planet (combating global warming).[19] Although some of these are clearly intangible, tree planting promoters make an effort to show that many other benefits *are* quantifiable, particularly the economic and environmental benefits. For example, the National Arbor Day Foundation has emphasized the contribution that trees make to property and home values and agricultural returns.

American Forests has highlighted how businesses can profit from sponsorship of and association with tree planting. And all three major groups—the nonprofit tree planting organizations, the timber industry, and the government—have taken to providing formulas for determining how much atmospheric carbon is sequestered by a tree or a forest. Inasmuch as carbon is a key feature of global warming, this seems to be a critical issue and one that lends itself to environmental appeals. There are many reasons to question the simplistic equation "more trees = less carbon = slower global warming," but questions do not seem to trouble the tree planting advocates, at least not yet.[20] American Forests offers interactive on-line calculators that determine how many trees an individual should plant to offset various activities, such as an airplane flight or a summer vacation trip taken in a car. The Environmental Protection Agency also offers a gauge for determining how much carbon generation can be offset by tree planting.

On a grander scale, International Paper, the largest private owner of timberland in North America, ran an advertising campaign saying, "If the world is warming, managed forests may be the best thermostat."[21] The ad goes on to note that International Paper plants more than 50 million trees annually. The concept of gaining pollution credits for tree planting, whether in the United States or abroad, has become a central element in international environmental treaty negotiations, first under the Clinton administration and then the Bush administration. Tree planting is thus advocated as a way to have both traditional economic growth and environmental health simultaneously.

The many benefits of trees will be explored in the following chapters. These attributes fall into several general categories (although there is considerable overlap): benefits to the environment, benefits to the economy, enhanced local beauty, and an enhanced sense of community. Trees are also considered a means for commemoration, and, for lack of a better term, for enhanced personal growth. There is remarkable agreement about what trees can do—what one group poses as a benefit, the others adopt and endorse as a benefit too. As described by Dianne Rocheleau and Laurie Ross, "Trees and forests have been turned into metaphors for the green dreams of global environmentalists, the green greed of multinational corporations, and the greening of popular movements."[22] It is striking that this shared mechanism—trees—can provide such wide-ranging interest groups with a vehicle of common cause.

TREES AS POLITICAL TOOLS

At this point I want to turn to the motivations for making such claims and suggest a theoretical outlook that helps to explain what the manipulation of trees, as well as the broader conceptions of stewardship and nature, is about. To do this, I draw upon the work of a number of scholars, many of them commonly associated with Marxist critiques of capitalism, and others who study constructions and interpretations of nature.

Though my interest is not in the mechanics of class struggle, I want to focus on the broad influence of the tree planting agenda across economic and political categories. To that end, the writing of the Italian scholar Antonio Gramsci (1891–1937) influences my work, in particular his theorization of the concept of hegemony.[23] One of Gramsci's primary goals was to solve the puzzle of working-class acquiescence in the face of domination and exploitation. Following Marxism, Gramsci anticipated that advanced capitalism, as found in Italy at the time he was writing, would lead to revolution by the working class. When that revolution failed to materialize, Gramsci felt challenged to explain how society held together, how it preserved its form and modus vivendi, in the face of fundamental problems that *should* have led "the masses" to seek radical change.

In essence, he wanted to examine and explain key modes of power, and he identified two types of control exercised by the coalition of government and ruling classes. The first type, direct domination, was that achieved through brute force, while the second, of greater interest to Gramsci and of particular note here, was hegemony, the persuasion, or enlistment of the cooperation, of the dominated classes. In effect, through the organs of civil society, the work of intellectuals, and the normalizing processes of cultural education, people are encouraged not only to accept the power structure but also to feel themselves a part of it.

Though Gramsci's work concerned politics and power in fascist Italy specifically, and Marxist revolution more broadly, his concept of hegemony is an important tool in analyzing the tree planting agenda in the United States. According to Dominic Strinati, "Hegemony operates culturally and ideologically through the institutions of civil society which characterize mature liberal-democratic, capitalist societies. These institutions include education, the family, the church, the mass media, popular culture, etc."[24] In other words, groups such as the National Arbor Day Foundation and American Forests may be seen as providing a conduit for the normalizing discourse that enlists Americans in a culture that speaks about environmental stewardship but does not fundamentally address the tension between capitalist views of nature and the welfare of the planet.

What then, we must ask, is the purpose and import of this discourse, and how does it serve to enlist and bind the participants in the hegemony of American capitalist life and its version of environmental stewardship? The power of language and image and their role in directing actions and belief are common themes in the analysis of popular and political culture. When it comes to the environment, the discourse is in part generated by and channeled through a range of interested participants, including scientists, academics, teachers, government bureaucrats, and not least, politicians—and the interest groups and donors that support them. What emerges from this coalition of voices is often perceived not as opinion or policy, however, but as "knowledge."[25] The work of the French philosopher Michel Foucault drew attention to what he termed power/knowledge, exploring the way language and institutions shape how people think and influence the questions that we ask, the problems we identify, and the solutions we contemplate.[26] The geographer David Demeritt argues that, in order to forestall protests about the widespread timber cutting in the United States as it was occurring, forests were cast in scientific terms and quantified in order to facilitate their management.[27] The scientific approach encouraged a distance between the "lay public" and the forest, as the natural world increasingly became something to be studied, managed, and taught about by a cadre of experts rather than experienced firsthand. The producers of the scientific and managerial discourse thus became even better positioned to shape public perceptions of the forest and of nature more broadly.

At the core of the planters' discourse is the premise that trees are good, and that planting them makes a multifaceted contribution to just about everything and everyone. To the degree that this premise seems logical, to the extent that tree planting is normalized as a virtuous act, it serves to advance the working of a hegemonic view of nature and the environment. The key, then, is to examine the genesis, dissemination, and perpetuation of this "common sense." I therefore explore the material concerning tree planting at the point where it is offered, or perhaps served, to the public. Here, the language of tree planting does its work, and we find it in all forms of daily communication. I argue that we are being bombarded by a growing stream of information that tells us to plant trees in order to improve, restore, repair, and perhaps even perfect the world around us.

Along with the common language, there is an element of practical cooperation that facilitates the hegemonic effort. The timber companies help the tree planting organizations, as does the government, which also helps timber companies that are supported by tree planting organizations. At the center of this constellation, I place groups such as American Forests and the National Arbor Day Foundation—not because they are the most powerful but because they serve as the most direct (and seductive) link between all three sectors and the general population. Thus I examine the mutual support between the sectors that accompanies the joint discursive platform deployed by those who plant trees while telling us how good they (the trees and the planters) are.

This message begins in grade school and youth organizations, where tree planting is linked with civic duty, local and national identity, beautification, and environmental health. Children are encouraged to identify with the trees they plant, to appreciate the long-term investment that comes with the life of a healthy tree, and to take pride in the stewardship that the planting represents. The primary expression of these sentiments comes in Arbor Day celebrations, but trees are regular characters in the classroom throughout the year (see figs. 3 and 4).

The tree planting message is directed at the post-school and post–

Figure 3. Arbor Day in American popular culture was subject to satire during the nation's bicentennial year. MAD Magazine, no. 184. © 1976 E. C. Publications, Inc. All rights reserved. Used with permission.

Figure 4.   Grant Wood's depression-era painting *Arbor Day* portrays an idyllic image of the holiday. © Estate of Grant Wood/Licensed by VAGA, New York, N.Y.

youth group population through the civic tree planting activities typical of communities across America. Church congregations, Elks and Rotary Clubs, and other groups of various stripes gather to plant trees to beautify areas and gain local recognition. In my own community, trees have been planted in recent years by women's shelters, at-risk youth groups, and just about any collection of individuals—including tree lovers—drawing in many who have had little hands-on experience with "nature." Trees can be planted by proxy too, and where the National Arbor Day Foundation leaves off with "free" trees mailed to its members, American Forests picks up with trees that can be planted (by others) via phone or Website, by check or credit card, or by the purchase of consumer goods. Eddie Bauer, one of American Forests' biggest corporate sponsors, offers its customers an opportunity to contribute money to Global ReLeaf to plant trees: when customers make a purchase from Eddie Bauer's stores or catalogues, they may pay an extra dollar, which the company will then match. Eddie Bauer's publicity states that "Every Tree Counts," and it goes on to note the millions of dollars the company has contributed and millions of trees it has planted by facilitating and matching customer contributions.[28] There are many such programs now, and the green mantle that attracts Eddie Bauer is sought by the timber industry as well.

Many of the large timber firms and their trade associations have showcased their tree planting efforts in order to promote a pro-environment image. Their message, which boasts both the number of trees planted and the environmental benefit that they provide, is directed at the general populace, civic groups, and policy makers (i.e., regulatory and legislative bodies). At the same time, the timber industry is aware that a positive reputation directly affects profits, and for many smaller companies this is a matter of corporate life or death. Thus the industry invests considerable resources in public relations departments, community outreach projects, philanthropy, and media campaigns that draw public attention to the role it plays in environmental stewardship and how it supports tree planting groups.

Much cultural information about trees and tree planting originates outside of the timber industry, however. Johnny Appleseed, the nineteenth-century itinerant tree planter, is held up as an example of selfless devotion to others, while his opposite, the tree cutter Paul Bunyan, seems to have been eclipsed. Dr. Seuss took an environmental turn in his 1972 book and film *The Lorax*, a scathing critique of rapacious greed in the guise of industrial production and consumerism.[29] More recently, the Republican National Committee urged its congressional candidates to boost their 1996 election campaigns by being photographed planting a tree, apparently an activity as American as apple pie.

DISCOURSES OF NATURE

At a broader level, the tree planting discourse contributes to and simultaneously taps into the powerful relationship that American culture—

and every other culture—has with nature. The concept of nature is remarkably complex, and I will not explore it at any great length here,[30] but it would be a mistake to suggest that the manipulation of images, language, and values that surrounds tree planting is unique. There are many other arenas in which issues of nature are contested. National parks, national forests, wilderness areas; the protection of baby seals, whales, and other creatures; and the local park all provide opportunities to embrace, define, and fight over nature.

The environmental historian William Cronon captures some of the tension inherent in contests over nature in his essay "The Trouble with Wilderness." Cronon, Roderick Nash, and many others identify wilderness as fundamental in popular American conceptions of nature and as a counterpoint to the negative image of modern industrial life.[31] Cronon finds an interesting role for the tree: it promotes a healthy concept of nature in a society that feels itself ever further removed from wilderness. He suggests,

> The tree in the garden is in reality no less other, no less worthy of our wonder and respect, than the tree in an ancient forest that has never known an ax or a saw—even though the tree in the forest reflects a more intricate web of ecological relationships. The tree in the garden could easily have sprung from the same seed as the tree in the forest, and we can claim only its location and perhaps its form as our own. Both trees stand apart from us; both share our common world.

In the garden tree, Cronon finds a deeper context for the duality of a planted tree and the "wild" tree. He believes that, as a representative of nature and wilderness, the garden tree "can help us perceive and respect a nature we had forgotten to recognize as natural" and thus "become part of the solution to our environmental dilemmas rather than part of the problem."[32] Yet it is often the case that planting trees, rather than truly connecting with nature, serves as a mechanism for dominating nature. For even if the planted tree grows according to its own design, its function is packaged and promoted within the context of environmental manipulation. Such manipulation draws upon deep-seated concepts of nature, including the idea that human beings are able to repair or improve nature's flaws;[33] thus I argue that trees offer a particularly powerful and intimate way to support or generate a hegemonic orientation toward nature and the environment.

According to the geographer David Harvey, "All proposals concerning 'the environment' are necessarily and simultaneously proposals for social change[,] and . . . action upon them always entails the instantiation in 'nature' of a certain regime of values."[34] Others join Harvey in linking nature and environment with politics and economics in an inextricable relationship, suggesting that, since the Enlightenment, Western cultures have viewed themselves as apart from and above nature. The post-Enlightenment orientation toward nature has been one of mastery and domination. Along with this stance comes the premise that, by dominating nature, human beings are able to dominate other people through, with, and for profit. This thesis is advanced by a range of writers, some of them drawing upon the work of Karl Wittfogel, who sought to demonstrate how societies can organize around the use of natural resources (water, in his thesis) in a manner that leads them to a despotic civilization binding together the control of resources and of the population.[35] Wittfogel writes of the coercive use of force; but, to return to Gramsci, the discourse of nature and trees that I pursue is less direct in its hegemonic orientation, though it, too, serves the accumulation of capital.

"The right of humanity to engage in extensive environmental modifications is tacitly accepted as sacrosanct," according to Harvey. He goes on to argue that in advanced capitalist societies:

> A powerful and persuasive array of discourses are embedded (sometimes without even knowing it) within this . . . view [of the environment] and its associated practices, institutions, beliefs, and powers. Environmental economics, environmental engineering, environmental law, planning and policy analysis, as well as a wide range of scientific endeavours[,] are ranged broadly in support of it. Such discourses are perfectly acceptable to the dominant forms of political-economic power precisely because there is no challenge implied within them to the hegemony of capital accumulation. Financial and logistical support therefore flows from the state and corporations to those promoting such environmental discourses, making them distinctive discourses of power.[36]

As Harvey suggests, many diverse participants can be implicated in contributing to and using a hegemonic discourse of trees, both knowingly and unknowingly. This particular discourse of trees as a panacea also draws strength from parallel or nested discourses (such as those of nature and the environment). That it does so is a critical point, for this helps to explain the involvement and complicity of well-intentioned people who think they are acting on behalf of the environment. Eric Darier points out that,

> since any action is situated in a specific context of power relations, it is possible to know if, tactically and at a given time, a Green act of resistance merely legitimizes the existing system of power relations or if it undermines it. Because of the extreme fluidity and adaptivity of the relations of power, a genuine act of Green resistance yesterday could rapidly become one of the legitimating elements for environmental practices contrary to the intentions of the initial acts of resistance. For example, the quest for scientific knowledge about the functioning of the natural environment can be seen as an instrument for instigating changes in human practices which might otherwise have arguably dire ecological and human consequences. However, the same knowledge can also be used to justify the introduction of changes in social practices vis-à-vis the "environment" which, in the longer term, could have even worse ecological and/or human consequences.[37]

If this is true of those who are seemingly engaged in acts of resistance, then it is an even greater concern for those in the mainstream who do things—like plant trees—that have become part of our cultural iconography. It is not that tree planting is harmful to the environment, but that tree planting provides a proxy. The act substitutes cosmetic physical changes that are morally satisfying for the radical reorganization of society and culture that would address the underlying attitudes and actions that have led to such widespread degradation of the natural and human world.

Before exploring the tree planters and their discourse, I want to offer a brief comment on my own relationship with trees. It feels somewhat odd for me to do this, but there have been those who confuse my critique of the tree planting discourse with hostility toward tree planting, tree planters, or even trees. I too love trees and plant them whenever I can, often reviewing as I do the many benefits they will provide. My deeper interest, however, is in institutions, patterns, and cultural and political mechanisms, and my concern is for the environment and our relations within it. My study is not directed at individuals, organizations, or even corporations that plant trees, though I criticize many of them, but rather at human arrogance and our sense of authority with respect to the environment, and the complacency this sense of authority fosters. Our propensity to focus on simple solutions for symptoms rather than tackle root causes is an impulse that ultimately will harm us and the trees we plant. In the chapters that follow, I explore the problematic elements of the tree planting discourse as it is woven by and between the protagonists I have identified as key participants in its construction.

THE TREE PLANTING TALE

Though my focus is contemporary, I begin by describing some of the historical roots of American tree planting, touching upon precolonial timber needs, the development of tree planting as an expression of patriotism, and the rise of charismatic tree planters. In the nineteenth century, the notion that "rain follows the plow" went hand in hand with large-scale tree planting across the Great Plains. In 1872, J. Sterling Morton established the Arbor Day holiday, which he went on to spread throughout the country. In many ways this is the starting point of the tree planting thread of the American environmental discourse, as schools, professional and hobby journals, and the popular press collaborated to establish tree planting as both a civic and a patriotic act encouraged by society. In 1875, the American Forests organization was founded, and it soon took an important place in the early development of national forest policy.

In Chapter 3, I examine the National Arbor Day Foundation, which was created to expand the institution of Arbor Day. The organization capitalizes on the popularity of the holiday and centralizes the administration of its observance; it is also responsible for expanding the one-day celebration to a year-round concern with conservation. Current National Arbor Day Foundation materials and programs that promote tree planting demonstrate the adversarial relationship between humans and nature that is promulgated under the guise of engaging with the environment, on the one hand, and advocating a human role in improving a benevolent yet damaged nature, on the other.

Chapter 4 takes a look at the American Forests organization's shift in orientation, to a "greener" message and policy, picking up the narrative of its history in 1972, with the inauguration of the National Arbor Day Foundation. My examination concentrates on the Global ReLeaf program, the flagship activity for American Forests since the mid-1990s. I detail the organizational weakness and lack of direction that preceded, and in some respects gave rise to, the now successful Global ReLeaf program. Using a range of American Forests' materials, including their journal, official histories, internal documents, and interviews, I explore the metaphors of nature that assign agency over the environment to the stewards—that is, to those who plant trees. In examining Global ReLeaf's corporate partnership program, I reveal just how broad the team of environmental stewards can be, and how easy it is to rent or purchase a place on American Forests' roster of green virtue.

Chapter 5 traces the flow of discourse and money that runs from U.S. Forest Service programs geared toward tree care and planting in communities throughout the United States (i.e., urban forestry). By providing both financial and technical support, the Forest Service influences the state foresters who work in each state, and the state foresters, in turn, distribute money and material to local government forestry agents. After following the chain of money and language from the federal to the local level, I address the locally based nonprofit tree planting groups that connect the government and national tree organizations—such as the National Arbor Day Foundation and American Forests—with the general public. I also discuss how the federal government, via the Forest Service and other means, supports nonprofit tree planters.

Chapter 6 begins with the history of the Forest Service as an agent of timber production on public lands. The Forest Service has a vested interest in the planting discourse, as it can justify the harvest of trees, and its broader mission as steward of commercial forests, only by demonstrating its ability to grow trees in a manner that negates the effects of cutting trees. The timber and paper products industries partner with the government in cutting and planting on public land and are the forest agents on private land. To explore the role of the timber industry in the tree planting discourse and its broader hegemonic interest, I draw upon the material disseminated in pursuit of a positive public image. The timber industry conveys both the idea that it modifies nature in a positive way and the idea that it is beneficent in relation to other organizations—like American Forests and the National Arbor Day Foundation—which share a similar perspective, even if for ostensibly conflicting reasons. I show that tree planting has been a standard element of the timber industry's green campaign, and that support of tree planting groups has become another popular avenue of corporate image building. I also look at the particular environmental claims that the timber companies make about their tree planting, and I contextualize them within the broader effects of timber harvesting and the scientific debates that swirl around the industry.

The concluding chapter synthesizes the message of the three primary planting sectors and collateral sources and interprets that synthesis in terms of a hegemonic view of the environment. I analyze the accuracy and efficacy of claims made about trees against the historical discourse and current science. The idea of a forest or environmental crisis in America is not new, nor is the notion that such conditions can be managed through programs such as tree planting. Indeed, though the ramifications of environmental modification grow, the attitudes and quick-fix orientations remain the same. Ultimately, despite the value of many of the trees planted for a variety of reasons and by a host of individuals and groups, the discourse that comes along with the trees merits deep concern.

More broadly, I illustrate the mechanism through which capital interests maintain our fundamental orientation toward nature without resort to force. The concept of hegemony is widespread, as is its casual use in the discussion of politics. My research is a more thorough examination of the way that hegemonic discourses are generated and deployed. The planting discourse is one way in which the public is incorporated into a hegemonic system that preserves the status quo with respect to the environment, even as it claims to bring about both change and effective indi-

vidual action via tree planting. Only after such discourses and their hegemonic purposes are revealed can serious critique be undertaken and the
threat to nature fully apprehended. Finally, I offer some thoughts that
may help to distance trees from the politicization that increasingly marks
their planting. Perhaps these thoughts can be considered while the shovel
prepares the holes for the next round of seedlings.

TWO Planting Patriotism, Cultivating Institutions

> If our ancestors found it wise and necessary to cut
> down vast forests, it is all the more needful that their
> descendants should plant trees. We shall do our part,
> therefore, towards awakening again, that natural love
> of trees, which this long warfare against them—this
> continual laying the axe at their roots . . . has, in so
> many places, well nigh extinguished.
>
> Andrew Jackson Downing, 1847

One of the earliest and most influential commentators on environmental issues in America was the naturalist and diplomat George Perkins Marsh, whose treatise *The Earth as Modified by Human Action* is often viewed as the foundational work of its kind. First published in 1863, the book was a clarion call for stewardship and preservation. In discussing American forests, Marsh said:

> The creation of new forests . . . is generally recognized, wherever the subject has received the attention it merits, as an indispensable measure of sound public economy. Enlightened individuals in some European states, the Governments in others, have made extensive plantations, and France, particularly, has now set herself energetically at work to restore the woods in her southern provinces, and thereby to prevent the utter depopulation and waste with which that once fertile soil and genial climate are threatened.

   The objects of the restoration of the forest are as multifarious as the
motives that have led to its destruction, and as the evils which that
destruction has occasioned. It is hoped that the replanting of the mountain slopes, and of bleak and infertile plains, will diminish the frequency
and violence of river inundations, prevent the formation of new torrents
and check the violence of those already existing, mitigate the extremes of
atmospheric temperature, humidity, and precipitation, restore dried-up
springs, rivulets and sources of irrigation, shelter the fields from chilling
and from parching winds, arrest the spread of miasmatic effluvia, and,
finally, furnish a self-renewing and inexhaustible supply of material
indispensable to so many purposes of domestic comfort.[1]

I cite Marsh at length because his writing eloquently captures a turning
point in American history and reflects much—both implicitly and explicitly—that characterizes the ongoing saga of both the forest and the trees.
It is appropriate that Marsh's observations came from time spent in
Europe, as that continent is the source of Euro-American concepts of
forestry and the source of those people who effected the radical transformation of the American forests that so concerned him.

   This chapter explores the history of tree planting in the United States
and traces the genesis of Arbor Day and the American Forests organization. This overview reveals the tensions that frame American attitudes
toward forests and lays out the basic language of the dispute. Positions
such as preservationism and conservationism that continue to mark the
discussion of forests in the United States draw, knowingly and unknowingly, on debates that have swirled for more than a century and that continue today. The evolution of American Forests and the National Arbor
Day Foundation are best viewed against this background, though the history of tree planting in the United States is a worthy subject in its own
right.

FORESTS IN EARLY AMERICAN LIFE

The common chronicle of initial European colonization of North America
describes a set of attitudes toward the natural environment that come, on

the one hand, from a mix of European intellectual and religious thought and, on the other, from the practical exigencies of survival. This mix played out as a need and desire to tame or dominate nature, which at the time was largely made up of vast forests. People had negative perceptions of the forest, seeing it as a nuisance, a hindrance to agriculture, a place of evil, and a savage wilderness beyond the realm of (Christian) civilization, but also lusted for the resource potential represented by the vast number of trees.[2]

Both the negative and the positive perceptions encouraged rapid encroachment on the forest. Local need for timber initially was small, but there was an almost immediate export market, and the forests were rapidly incorporated into an expanding international economy. The refining of sugar in the Caribbean, which required a great deal of (imported) wood for fuel, the outfitting of English ships with masts, and the cooperage for many food products came to depend on a growing supply of timber from the forests of New England and the Atlantic coast. Competition for forest resources, already evident in the seventeenth century, intensified during the next century.[3] Indeed, according to Perlin, British efforts to control the American timber trade were a major precipitating cause of the struggle for independence.[4] Dependence on wood, both for domestic use and export revenues, was an obvious fact of existence, and not surprisingly the results of the assault on the forest affected the fabric of everyday life. Increasingly there were instances of shortage amid abundance. Already in 1745, Benjamin Franklin was "lamenting the scarcity of fuel that had formerly been 'at any man's door' and the need to bring wood from considerable distance to heat (and later house) the growing cities."[5] As the forest fell more rapidly to accommodate human consumption, the dynamic of the empire and its need for trees, seen elsewhere in the world, was under way in America as well.

THE FIRST EURO-AMERICAN TREE PLANTING

According to J. P. Kinney, tree planting in America was encouraged by government legislation as early as the 1624 session of the Colonial Assembly of Virginia, which directed property owners to plant mulberry trees in support of the silk trade. Thirty-two years later, another act of the assembly mandated planting various species of trees in proportion to the size of the landholding.[6] In addition to the utilitarian purposes that warranted tree planting, there were aesthetic motivations as well. Watson details the early use of trees for urban ornamentation, citing examples in the Boston Common, which was planted with English elms between 1723 and 1729, and after, American chestnuts in Georgetown in 1735 and in New Haven in 1760. He cites 1628 as the year for establishment of the first nursery in America, and 1630 for the second, and the use of tree names for street nomenclature in William Penn's territory in the 1680s.[7]

Planting trees and applying their names to other features of the human landscape reflect some of the affection people had for trees, a sentiment that stood alongside their antipathy or utilitarian attitudes toward the American forests. Individual trees, either planted or growing naturally, were objects of attention and affection and were linked to elements of civic and national pride. Particular trees were planted in honor of family members; others were accorded status based on their proximity to or function in notable events or on their ownership by famous people. Some of these trees remain alive today, though many have died, and many of them, either living or dead, have retained their fame.

One of these, Connecticut's Charter Oak, was recently commemorated in the series of twenty-five-cent coins issued by the U.S. Mint. The official tree of Connecticut, the Charter Oak has been a favorite symbol since before U.S. independence. The state advertises the tree with time-honored hyperbole: "Deep-rooted in the historic tradition of Connecticut, the Charter Oak is one of the most colorful and significant symbols of the spiritual strength and love of freedom which inspired our colonial forebears in their militant resistance to tyranny."[8] Veneration is accorded to the tree as a result of its longevity (it perished in 1856 at the age of several hundreds of years), but primarily for its service as the hiding place for the charter given to Governor John Winthrop by King Charles II of England in 1662.[9] Trees have not had to play such an active role to accrue status, however. In 1999, the last of the Liberty Trees in Annapolis, Maryland, was cut down, the final member of the group that shaded the Sons of Liberty as they plotted their resistance to British rule.[10]

Trees served the Euro-Americans in a host of ways and were imbued with a variety of meanings and cultural roles, some new, others traditional. Early American history is far more a history of the consumption of trees and the widespread clearing of forests than a chronicle of tree planting. It is clear, however, that both naturally growing and planted trees were elements of the landscape of settled areas, and they were considered providential in view of the increasing localized shortages, particularly of fuelwood. Thus, from the earliest days of European settlement, and from the first decades of American Independence, the population demonstrated a mixture of utilitarian and aesthetic orientations toward trees.

PLANTING FOR ENVIRONMENTAL ALTERATION

By the mid–nineteenth century it was difficult to ignore the enormous inroads that had been made in American forests, and concern was increasingly voiced over the fate of the forest—and all that was attached to it. People were also concerned about the quality of life in the growing towns in the East and, as westward migration swelled, the physical aspects of new areas of (white) settlement. The rapidly changing dynamics of the American landscape led to calls for tree planting in both the public and the private sectors, and many of the mechanisms brought to the task provided templates for tree planting efforts still in use.

As settlement patterns and economic activities diversified and grew more complex, the utility of trees was appreciated across a wide— though not necessarily large—segment of the population. As a result, tree planting was frequently encouraged, even urged, by local, state, and federal government officials, horticulturalists, and commentators on the environment. J. P. Kinney's list of tree planting legislation in American history is impressive because of both the number of such laws and their coverage.[11] Tree planting was mandated to stimulate agriculture, provide shade, promote beautification, and for various other ends. Yet despite the regularity of such efforts, compulsory tree planting seems to have been a consistently unenforceable way to achieve these goals. In the mid–

nineteenth century and after, this contributed to a chorus of lament over the state of the environment and the fate of nature.

In 1867, the state of Wisconsin commissioned Increase Latham to write the *Report on the Disastrous Effects of the Destruction of Forest Trees Now Going On So Rapidly in the State of Wisconsin.*[12] In it, Latham discusses the deleterious environmental and economic effects of forest clearing in other countries and other times, tapping into the existing perspective of the rise and fall of empires. Latham advocated tree planting to ameliorate some of the forest devastation caused by timber cutting and fires. Other examples of devastation prompted a similar response. Richard Lillard notes an upswing in tree planting in the wake of the Civil War that occurred partly in response to the timber shortages it created or exacerbated.[13] Marsh's work was circulating at this time as well, and it paralleled the concerns of Latham and others.

Some of these authors married the concern for the forest with a growing general appreciation of nature and the aesthetics of the American landscape in particular. Notable among these was the famous writer and editor of the *Horticulturalist and Journal of Rural Art and Rural Taste,* Andrew Jackson Downing, who is also author of the epigraph that opens this chapter.[14] Downing wanted to recast both the American landscape and the American people, and to this end he sought to enlist individuals, nurserymen, horticultural societies, and others. His goal was to stimulate tree planting both for the intrinsic value of the trees, particularly ornamental trees, and for practical reasons, including the growth of the horticulture industry.

In 1847 he noted, "Pleasure and profit are certain, sooner or later, to awaken a large portion of our countrymen to the advantages of improving their own private grounds."[15] He was vehement about the need to plant trees, observing that America's towns and villages were "in a shameless state of public nudity and neglect."[16] Downing deployed flowery biblical images in his work and the sort of moral tone that was, and still is, often featured in disputes over nature.[17] Treeless cities were likened to Sodom, and he went so far as to say that "no one who has sense enough rightly to understand the wonderful system of life, order, and harmony, that is involved in one of our grand and majestic forest-trees, could ever destroy it, unnecessarily, without a painful feeling, we should say, akin at least to murder in the fourth degree."[18] Tree planters— the righteous—were to be supported, and Downing called for the distribution of free trees to stimulate their work and encourage others to join in the task. According to Downing, there was an "army" of several hundred thousand Americans doing their "patriotic duty" in planting trees, but that was not a sufficient number. "Let every man, whose soul is not a desert, plant trees," was his call to arms.[19]

MAKING RAIN ON THE PLAINS

Like Downing, who hoped for a transformation of the American landscape, settlers in the Great Plains wanted to change their surroundings. They saw, and were encouraged to appreciate, tree planting as the means to accomplish this task—and more. As settlement pushed from the still-forested East into the open plains, the lack of trees became an immediate obstacle. While trees had been seen as a barrier to agriculture in New England and the Atlantic coast, on the plains their absence was acknowledged as a critical challenge primarily for two reasons. First, there was the dearth of wood and, consequently, wood products such as railroad fuel and track ties.[20] Second, the lack of trees raised questions about whether the soil and climate were suitable for agriculture, since it was commonly believed that the presence of forests connoted fertile soil, and that their absence reflected sterile earth. Moreover, it was believed that a lack of trees was partly responsible for the lack of rainfall. The way to address these challenges, or so people thought, was to plant trees.

This view of environmental alteration had originated in discussions about deforestation in the East. There, deforestation had led to degraded soils and was thought to have caused a drop in rainfall. Marsh articulated these ideas in relation to forest loss, and those who calculated the inverse benefits—the gains that would come with replacing or creating a forest—adopted his work. The idea that "rain follows the plow" was conceptually joined by "rain follows the tree," and Walter Kollmorgen calls Marsh's *Man and Nature* the "bible of the rainmakers of the west."[21]

He cites the U.S. commissioner of agriculture, who praised a tree plant-ing program initiated by the state of Kansas for its potential to increase the population of the state, raise property values, moderate climatic extremes, and aid in the cultivation of crops.[22]

John Ise comments that it "may seem strange that interest should have developed regarding the planting of new trees before there was any general interest in the preservation of forests already grown; but without doubt the matter of tree planting was of greater interest in the early [1870s] than any other object relating to forestry."[23] Support for tree plant-ing was forthcoming at both the state and federal levels. Again, tree planting was cast as a patriotic act with benefits for both the individual and the nation. Supporting the move to plant trees on the Great Plains, at least in theory, was the Timber Cultures Act of 1873.[24] This federal legis-lation addressed the shortage of timber on the Great Plains by offering a land-for-trees deal also seen as a key tool for improving the climate through increased rainfall. Barron McIntosh cites Senator Phineas W. Hitchcock, the bill's sponsor, as saying, "The object of this bill is to encourage the growth of timber, not merely for the benefit of the soil, not merely for the value of the timber itself, but for its influence upon the cli-mate."[25] Modeled on the Homestead Act, the Timber Cultures Act offered 160 acres of land in return for the dedication of one-quarter of that land to tree growing. It stipulated that trees be planted not more than twelve feet apart and that they be kept healthy and growing for a period of at least ten years.[26]

Ultimately the Timber Cultures Act—abused by land speculators, manipulated by homesteading families, and doomed by the difficulty of growing trees with little available water—was deemed a failure and repealed in 1891. There is evidence that millions of trees were planted under this Act, but there is also evidence that the goals articulated in the Act were not met. Save for local exceptions, the wood shortage was not assuaged, soil was not stabilized, and rainfall was not induced. Despite this, tree planting remained popular, and this was reflected in supportive legislation enacted by states in several regions.

Though unable to provide land in exchange for tree planting, state governments could offer financial incentives. Some furnished bounties for trees, such as the two dollars per acre Kansas proffered in 1868 for trees grown for a period of three years. In 1867, Minnesota offered a prize for the best five acres of cultivated timber.[27] Some Eastern states took the approach of giving tax breaks for land put into and kept in timber cultivation. Maine established a twenty-year tax break for land successfully growing two thousand or more trees per acre for at least three years. Connecticut residents were required to establish twelve hundred trees per acre at a height of greater than six feet to qualify for a ten-year tax exemption, but the state limited the benefit to those who grew chestnut, locust, hickory, ash, catalpa, white oak, sugar maple, European larch, white pine, or spruce. Massachusetts's program, which also required two thousand trees per acre, measuring four feet or greater, offered a tax break for any type of pine. Policies of this kind, enacted in states around the country, continued well into the twentieth century.

THE GENESIS OF ARBOR DAY

Coincident with the spread of government-supported tree planting programs was the popularization of planting efforts among citizens whose interest in trees may have included, but was certainly not limited to, timber production. Whether they sought to enhance their crops, modify the climate, or beautify their towns, they promoted tree planting as a means by which individuals could make a positive contribution. J. Sterling Morton (1832–1903), the founder of Arbor Day, tapped into this sentiment.

Morton was not the first to become famous as an American tree planter; that distinction goes to John Chapman (1774–1845), commonly known as Johnny Appleseed. Chapman was born in Massachusetts and spent much of his life distributing apple seeds and seedlings throughout remote areas of Pennsylvania, Ohio, Indiana, and elsewhere. His goal was to provide settlers with both nutrition and a means for economy, and to spread the teachings of Swedenborgian Christianity. The myth of Johnny Appleseed added a patina of charity to his considerable efforts. Such historiography contributes to the reverence that characterizes accounts of his and Morton's work.[28]

Morton's goal was more ambitious than Chapman's: he sought to institutionalize tree planting in every sector of American life. His public career was a combination of agriculture, journalism, and politics. The three complemented one another in nineteenth-century Nebraska, as agriculture was the base of the economy, journalism promoted settlement activities in the territory and its growth, and politics allocated the rewards that came along with that growth. Each branch of Morton's work supported the other two. Though biographers depict him primarily as a farmer and politician, Morton was in many respects a promoter.

Like others in his time and place, Morton saw the need to make Nebraska a more productive environment for settlers, and he saw trees as one way to achieve this end. As a farmer, he perceived all the utilitarian benefits—real and imagined—they could provide. For Morton, planting trees came to represent a gain for the individual and a civic duty. No stranger to chauvinism and hyperbole, he portrayed this duty as a means of betterment. Remarks to the Horticultural Society of Nebraska capture his tone:

> Orchards are missionaries of culture and refinement. They make the people among whom they grow a better and more thoughtful people. If every farmer in Nebraska will plant out and cultivate an orchard and a flower garden, together with a few forest trees, this will become mentally and morally the best agricultural state, the grandest community of producers in the American union. Children reared among trees and flowers growing up with them will be better in mind and heart, than children reared among hogs and cattle.[29]

Thus it was to improve the people of his state that Morton advocated organized tree planting on a vast scale.

He began his arboreal evangelism while editor of the *Nebraska City News,* where, in addition to promoting settlement in the territory, he offered counsel on cultivating orchards and planting trees for a variety of other purposes. His words came at a time of growing appreciation for tree planting: around the same time, the state offered several prizes for the most trees planted. Morton wanted a broader effort, however, and the State Board of Agriculture, of which he was a member, adopted his resolution marking April 10, 1872, as the first Arbor Day. That resolution reads:

Resolved, That Wednesday, the 10th day of April, 1872, be, and the same is hereby, especially set apart and consecrated for tree planting in the State of Nebraska, and the State Board of Agriculture hereby name it Arbor Day; and to urge upon the people of the State the vital importance of tree planting, hereby offer a special premium of one hundred dollars to the agricultural society of that county in Nebraska which shall, upon that day, plant properly the largest number of trees; and a farm library of twenty-five dollars' worth of books to that person who, on that day, shall plant properly, in Nebraska, the greatest number of trees.

Morton marked the observance of the holiday with particularly senti-mental language, saying, "The cultivation of trees is the cultivation of the good, the beautiful, and the ennobling in man, and for one, I wish to see this culture become universal in the State."[30] Trees were also a feature of an egalitarian democracy, he argued: "The poorest landowner in Nebraska has just as large a fortune, of time, secured to him, as the rich-est. And the rain and sunshine and seasons will be his partners, just as genially and gently as they will be those of any millionaire, and will make the trees planted by the poor man grow just as grandly and beau-tifully as those planted by the opulent."

It has been widely noted that over 1 million trees were planted throughout Nebraska on the first Arbor Day, and the holiday was soon adopted by other states and countries. The Nebraska State Legislature honored Morton in 1885 by designating his birthday, April 22, as the annual date of Arbor Day observance and a state holiday. The rapid spread of Arbor Day beyond Nebraska deserves some attention, but before turning to that phenomenon, a few words are in order about the tenor of Morton's rhetoric.

Like much of Morton's promotional work, and typical of that genre, the plans for and descriptions of Arbor Day are marked by grandiosity and ambition. On the one hand, Morton's enthusiasm is borne out by the continuing success of Arbor Day and the many trees (tens of millions at least, though it would be impossible to count) that have been planted in conjunction with its observance. On the other hand, tree planting has not changed the climate of the Great Plains, and it has not fundamentally altered the economy of Nebraska, let alone wider territories. The disjunction between the vision of Arbor Day's architect and the actual benefits of tree planting is not the exception, however. Rather, it is a pattern that was quickly picked up by other promoters of trees and carried down to the present day. Morton was a promoter of an ascendant America, and though he did not specifically articulate a grand hegemonic design in his advocacy of tree planting, his hyperbole has provided a template for both those who generate the discourse of trees and those who subscribe to it.

THE SPREAD OF ARBOR DAY

Arbor Day began as a celebration sponsored in part by governmental bodies and disseminated via newspapers and local boosters, but it quickly entered into the realm of education. A decade after the first Arbor Day, a national forestry convention in Cincinnati called upon schoolchildren to plant trees in memorial groves dedicated to famous figures in American history. That ceremony was widely publicized, and the following year a forestry committee meeting in St. Paul recommended that schools throughout the country celebrate Arbor Day. By 1892, a committee of the National Education Association noted the observance of Arbor Day in schools in forty states and territories.[31] Charles Skinner, compiler of the *Arbor Day Manual: An Aid in Preparing Programs for Arbor Day Exercises,* felt that Arbor Day was "rapidly becoming one of the most interesting and one of the most extensively observed of school holidays."[32] He cites an 1889 article in the Richfield Springs, N.Y., school paper *The Student* that describes trees: "As modifiers of the climate, trees, woodlands, and forest-tracts are not justly appreciated. They cool the atmosphere, and so temper the extremes of climatic 'fickleness,' that they become somewhat more endurable. They act as obstructions to destructive winds, which in event of the absence of forest-lands would sweep clear across unprotected districts. As beneficial to health, they stand preeminent."[33]

Though Morton's political record reflects more losses than victories, the spread of Arbor Day contributed to his stature, and he was appointed secretary of agriculture by President Grover Cleveland in 1892. It was during his tenure that Nathaniel Egleston, a U.S. Department of Agriculture employee, prepared a report for one of Morton's assistant secretaries titled *Arbor Day: Its History and Observance*. Egleston notes that Arbor Day had "become a national holiday and one of our important institutions,"[34] and he collected testimony to this effect from around the country, creating a model for celebrations of the celebration itself. He marshaled the comments of academics, politicians, professional foresters, clergy, educators, and "average citizens" to affirm the importance and nature of Arbor Day's observance. Typical of the entries in Egleston's compendium are the remarks of J. M. Carlisle, superintendent of public instruction for the state of Texas, who commented that, through Arbor Day, "the sentiment in favor of both physical and moral cleanliness is greatly strengthened, while patriotic feelings are aroused and the people are drawn together by the contemplation of so many great themes in which all have a common interest."[35] J. T. Rothrock, state commissioner of forestry for Pennsylvania and a leading figure in the early days of American silviculture, emphasized the benevolence of Arbor Day. In an 1895 speech reported by Egleston, he said tree planting would "exemplify the noble justice of leaving the world in as good condition for the prosperity of your children as you found it for yourselves. All this you may do by simply planting a tree, which will grow while you sleep and draw its strength and its long life and large usefulness from the sunshine and the storm, costing nothing, harming no one, blessing everyone, and pleasing God."[36]

Commemoration of Arbor Day seems to have become an industry in the late nineteenth and early twentieth centuries. Schools published manuals on Arbor Day observance, and school districts, ranging from the local to the state level, organized and facilitated the implementation of the Arbor Day programs. Notables frequently participated in school activities, both directly and by circulating their thoughts and remarks on trees and tree planting. Robert Schauffler's 1909 collection of Arbor Day material included a letter from Teddy Roosevelt to American schoolchildren, along with selections from Washington Irving, William Cullen Bryant, Walt Whitman, George Perkins Marsh, Gifford Pinchot, John Muir, and the noted environmentalist William Shakespeare.[37] Muir's comments sounded a discordant note, as he felt that planting trees would not "avail much toward getting back anything like the noble primeval forests."[38]

On the whole, however, the march of the holiday into the nation's schools and other public spheres was greeted with triumphal tones and laudatory words. Indeed, for well over a hundred years, trees have been promoted as environmental agents, and those who plant them have been commended as contributing to the common good. The "selfless" act of planting a tree has also been linked to patriotism: good citizenship is demonstrated by modifying nature through trees, a theme that has remained powerful since Morton elevated it in the public sphere.

THE BIRTH OF AMERICAN FORESTS

American Forests was created in 1875 as a result of concern for the forests that was driven by both excessive cutting and catastrophic fires. The organization was the brainchild of John Aston Warder, a physician, farmer, and pomologist (a specialist in apple cultivation) who, like Marsh, had been influenced by his exposure to European forestry. At the time of American Forests' birth, forestry as a formal profession had not yet been introduced in the United States, and environmental advocacy was yet to emerge as the work of national citizens groups. The writings of Marsh and others had contributed to growing alarm about the forests, and events such as the catastrophic Peshtigo fire demonstrated the need for action in addition to commentary.[39] Warder's new organization drew together concerned citizens—among them horticulturalists, botanists, academics, and nursery owners—who had some technical knowledge but little professional role in the management of forests.

The twin purposes of American Forests, as articulated at its inception, were to protect the forest from wanton destruction and to promote tree planting. Warder noted, "The government of a republic need not own forests, but by judicious enactments it may and should foster them where they belong, in the possession of the citizen, and by so doing the good of many will be conserved."[40] This quote charts the course of the organization, which appealed to private landowners and encouraged them to practice good stewardship in their forests. In addition, American Forests set out to define and advocate a governmental role in protecting forests on *public* lands, a position that anticipated the creation of the national forests and the U.S. Forest Service. Though I am mainly interested in the tree planting element of American Forests, it is necessary to devote some attention to forest protection, a primary focus of the organization.[41]

Tree planting, as envisioned by American Forests, had two distinct tracks. One was the planting of trees for ornamental and other nonindustrial purposes, and this appealed to the horticulturalists and nurserymen among the organization's membership. A second and more compelling reason for planting, as it was then articulated, was the stocking of forestland for timber purposes. The constituencies of these two tracks were markedly distinct, the first largely urban homeowners, the second primarily rural landowners, but in both cases predominantly male and of some means. This geographical bifurcation has marked American Forests for more than a hundred years and created tension in the effort to define the organization's mission and tailor it to the membership. In fact, the early years of American Forests were marked by little growth or activity, and, in 1882, the organization merged with the American Forestry Congress, a newly formed group influenced by Bernhard Fernow, a Prussian-born forester who had migrated to the United States in 1876.[42]

The merger did not fundamentally change the purpose of the organization, or its constituency. By 1899, American Forests' membership had grown only to 1,025, but many of those members were active in advocacy in Washington, D.C., and elsewhere. Reflecting this, in 1900 the organization moved its headquarters from a commercial space to the building housing the Department of Agriculture, where it could easily coordinate with Gifford Pinchot, then chief of the Forestry Division and, simultaneously, chair of American Forests' executive committee. Beyond the personal contacts that were part and parcel of Washington's political culture, the primary mechanism for conveying the views of the organization was its journal. The journal described its purpose as being "especially useful to lumbermen and owners of forest lands, parks, grounds, and others practically interested in arboriculture."[43] Titled *The Forester*, it was mailed to the membership and another five hundred or so readers. Inasmuch as only a limited number of members attended the annual meeting or participated in the workings of the organization, the journal served as the primary link between American Forests and its membership.

DEBATES OVER ADVOCACY AND POLICY

According to *The Forester*, the purpose of the organization was to promote:

1. A more rational and conservative treatment of the forest resources of this continent.
2. The advancement of educational, legislative and other measures tending to promote this object.
3. The diffusion of knowledge regarding the conservation, management, and renewal of forests, the methods of reforestation of waste lands, the proper utilization of forest products, the planting of trees for ornament, and cognate subjects of arboriculture.[44]

The journal was also a vehicle for expression of the views of the timber industry, through interviews with company officials, articles about or submitted by timber men, letters to the editor, and corporate advertisements. By 1910, the industry was alert to the limitations of America's timber supply (and the growing importance of public relations), and was speaking to concerns that it saw as being shared with the members of American Forests. A representative of the American Forest and Paper Association asserted, "The planting and growing of new forests is already an assured fact. Thus will be brought to the paper industry an inexhaustible supply of raw material from farm and field and from forests now grown and growing and forests hereafter to be planted and grown."[45] An advertisement from the National Lumber Manufacturers Association in 1928 reads remarkably like the current industry campaign. Under a picture of trees planted on clear-cut land (as they term it), the text reads, in part: "In conservation conversation it is frequently revealed that people think of all tree-felling as 'destruction' instead of utilization.

Uninformed enthusiasts talk of lumbering and paper-making as 'destructive'; they don't so talk of iron and steel making. The forests are renewable and have been renewing themselves for five million years."[46]

The tension between the goals of forest regulation formally articulated by American Forests and the self-defined interests of the timber industry led to conflict within the organization. In its orientation, American Forests started out on the side of conservationism (which advocated maintaining natural resources for ongoing use), in keeping with the views of Gifford Pinchot and others, rather than preservationism (which favored setting aside areas rather than using them) of the type associated with John Muir. Pinchot, who was active in American Forests, used his typically blunt terms concerning the forest and what conservation meant, a vision he felt the timber industry was sorely lacking:

> I have no interest whatever in the protection of the forest *per se*. Unless it serves some useful purpose, a standing forest appeals to me not at all (except from the merely aesthetic side). I want it distinctly understood that forest protection is to the forester a means, not an end. . . .
>
> The only thing which can be relied upon to protect [the timber industry] and the enormous interests which depend upon it is forestry. We must consider from now on that the forest is a crop; that methods of renewing it are just as vital to [those] who are interested in cutting it down, as to those who are interested in building it up.[47]

Pinchot's agenda for the forest differed from that of the timber industry and, increasingly, from that of American Forests, in that he advocated government regulation on public *and* private land to insure the timely regeneration of the trees. In the years around World War I, philosophical differences about the role of government erupted into a serious breach in the organization. On one side were professional foresters, those charged with managing the land. On the other side were owners from the timber industry and their sympathizers, and it was this second group who managed to dominate the leadership of American Forests from 1913 to 1922. Prior to that period, the organization had been active in policy advocacy and was seen as an important supporter of the government and, in particular, the Forest Service, a source for many of its leading members.

Under the leadership of Henry Drinker (1913–1915) and then Charles Lathrop Pack (1916–1922), however, American Forests began to move away from advocacy and took only "safe" positions, avoiding issues that aroused public controversy. This led many of the organization's longtime supporters in the ranks of professional forestry to condemn it for abandoning its raison d'être.

The split in the organization became public in 1921, when the disaffected members turned to the journal of the Society of American Foresters to air their grievances. In several editions of the journal, American Forests members, including a prominent member of the board of directors and a number of leading foresters, lashed out at the organization's leadership, especially President Pack. Their language was blunt and furious. In the first of a series of articles, Herman H. Chapman, a Yale professor and director of American Forests, wrote, "Today the [organization] stands completely discredited in the eyes of the entire body of professional foresters who are acquainted with the facts of its management, and only ignorance of these facts on the part of its members and the public preserves to it a shred of its former influence and usefulness."[48] Chapman's pique had begun during the presidency of Henry Drinker, and he cited Drinker's contention regarding federal regulation that "it is the duty of this body to teach and to urge the economic use and conservation of our natural resources whether they are located in Government, State, or private holdings, and not to become involved as partisans in any position of antagonism in political discussions of this nature."[49]

At issue was the fundamental question of the federal government's role in regulating forestry. Much of the leadership of American Forests during this period articulated the timber industry's position, and many of the organization's directors were hostile to the growing national forest system, and all the more so to a federal role on private lands. They pressed the case that, if there were to be regulation at all, it should be administered at the state level, where their influence was more keenly felt. The professional foresters saw in this position a challenge to important forestry practices and, thereby, to the role of the foresters in carrying out their duty.

In illuminating the dispute, Chapman detailed some of the affiliations and dispositions of other members of the American Forests board. He noted that Director Chester Lyman was the head of International Paper and suggested that he was "not fully awake to the public duty and responsibility of the Association, or also, of necessity, constrained by his business connections to consider all acts of the Association in the light of their effect on his corporate responsibilities."[50] Director W. R. Brown was identified as the owner of the Brown Corporation of New Hampshire, with large timber holdings and operations in New England and Canada, and a known enemy of the Forest Service. Director J. B. White was described as a man "very much interested in forest conservation everywhere except on his own operations, where it is unfortunately impossible owing to a number of good economic reasons."[51] Chapman then turned to the forest practices of President Pack, former head of the Pack Woods Company. He charged that "the cutting methods employed in stripping . . . timber from Mr. Pack's lands as witnessed . . . and photographed by me, constitute the worst examples of complete forest denudation in the South and cannot be exceeded in complete destructiveness anywhere in the United States."[52]

Though Chapman was the point man in the attack on Pack and his allies, there were many who supported his effort to reorient American Forests toward its earlier goals. The editors of the journal of the Society of American Foresters commented, "The American Forestry Association [i.e., American Forests] has lost its moral right to speak in the name of the public and of forestry."[53] One of the editors sadly lamented, "In the American Forestry Association the spirit of Fernow and Pinchot has died."[54]

Though some elements of this dispute revolved around mundane issues of personalities, budgets, salaries, and bylaws (the mechanics of organizational power), the political-philosophical aspects of the two sides represent important forces in the history of American Forests. Timber interests were, and remain, committed to limiting regulation of forestland and practices, and under Drinker and Pack, the organization broadcast those sentiments. During those years, professional foresters were often employed by or identified with the Forest Service, and they advocated an increased role for the government in managing both public and private land, a position echoed by the conservation movement as a whole. Over the intervening decades, the Society of American Foresters has moved much closer to the position of the timber industry, and American Forests has moved in the direction of the Forest Service, but that important exchange of roles comes later in the narrative.

American Forests quickly changed tack after the controversy of the Drinker-Pack years, appointing a professional forester, Ovid Butler, as executive secretary of the organization and electing Henry Graves as its head in 1923. Graves was dean of the Yale Forest School and a former chief of the Forest Service, and he counted William B. Greeley, then head of the Forest Service, among his friends. The two pushed for a larger role for the Forest Service and found allies in that effort in Congress. The Senate established a Select Committee on Reforestation, which, with the help of its supporters—prominent among them American Forests—successfully advocated passage of the Clarke-McNary Act in 1924. The Act promoted financial incentives for reforestation, extended the national forests, and promoted federal and state cooperation in forestry matters. Several years later, the timber industry published ads in the journal of American Forests, in which it claimed to be complying with the Act, drawing a stiff response from Pinchot, who protested the publication of what he felt were "direct and intentional misrepresentations of the situation, and [which] have for their purpose to mislead the reader."[55]

Such tensions continue to mark the relationship between the timber industry and the conservation movement today, and they have been played out, albeit with a varying constellation of partners, in the pages of American Forests' journal and the activities of the organization's directors and employees. Pinchot finally resigned from American Forests in 1943—for the second time—and his departure, as documented in the board's internal papers, was little lamented by Butler and some others. They walked the line separating the organization's differing constituencies, and had grown weary of Pinchot's stridency and aggressive stance on regulation. The question of regulation of timberland and the shifting alliances between the timber industry, the Forest Service, and the leadership of American Forests—and the tensions that have resulted—have been hallmarks of the organization's history.

PROMOTING TREES

American Forests was far more involved in education and dissemination of knowledge than in practical tree planting projects, though it did advocate Arbor Day celebrations and commemorative plantings. The organization devoted a significant amount of energy to practical decisions concerning individuals—for instance, what type of trees to plant in which soils, at which particular times. The journal gave considerable space to such issues, sometimes at the expense of discussions of policy questions. Authors and letter writers expressed powerful sentiments about trees, gave technical advice, and even, as early as the nineteenth century, proposed formulas for proper planting. The range of tree planting issues was broad and included the appropriate occasions and purposes for ceremonial tree planting, the importance of reforestation, the role of trees in conservation education, and so on.

After World War I, American Forests actively supported the planting of memorial trees around the country. Anyone planting a memorial tree—whether an individual or group—could receive a certificate of recognition from American Forests. The organization maintained a National Honor Roll of Memorial Trees, which was published in the journal several times a year. American Forests also promoted the planting of Mother's Day trees and supported Arbor Day celebrations in their many forms.

In fact, the journal celebrated tree planting of all kinds and showed appreciation for both individual and group efforts. The year 1928 was marked, for example, as the year in which the Boy Scouts planted 1 million trees.[56] In New York, 4-H Clubs planted 12 million trees over a decade, under the slogan "Young folks and trees grow up together."[57] An even larger New York project lauded by the journal was the proposal to plant 1 million acres of abandoned farmland with forest trees, and the tree planting efforts of the Civilian Conservation Corps (1933–1942), sometimes called the Tree Army, received broad coverage.[58] Over the next thirty years, American Forests was consistent in calling for reforestation on a massive scale, linking it to the tens of millions of acres of forestland that needed restocking.[59] As far as its own planting programs, however, the next big step came in 1972 with Tree Time USA, described in chapter 4.

FOUR CENTURIES OF TREE PLANTING

In this brief and incomplete survey of both tree planting and the institutions and individuals associated with it, a number of points stand out. First, tree planting is not a new phenomenon: from the earliest days of the European occupation of North America, trees have been planted for utilitarian, commemorative, and ceremonial purposes. Second, the link between the welfare of the forest and tree planting as a remedy has been commonly pointed out in discussions of nature and the environment in the United States. Third, charismatic individuals and organizations have worked to institutionalize the tree in American life. While Johnny Appleseed had a utilitarian and religious agenda, J. Sterling Morton and John Aston Warder sought to encourage tree planting for a wide range of benefits, not least of which was the connection between acting on behalf of the environment and the promotion of civic responsibility. Patriotism has been associated with trees throughout American history, and tree planters readily assume the image of moral good. This is possible in part because there has always been a call to plant more trees than are actually planted; thus the appeal is continual and always engaging.

Since the inception of Arbor Day in 1872 and American Forests in 1875, there has been an organized call for tree planting. I have sketched out the origins of both of these institutions in order to introduce the current work carried out by the National Arbor Day Foundation and American Forests. While my introduction necessarily has been brief, it demonstrates that there is a history of engaging nature through, and forming community around, tree planting, and that efforts of this type are designed, facilitated, and promoted by a cadre of dedicated individuals and their organizations. The planting programs that have resulted have been a meeting place— sometimes ephemeral and sometimes enduring—for teachers, students, government workers and officials, members of the timber industry, and other interested parties. There are also "official" agendas articulated by all participants and celebrated as instances of high purpose and common ground. The subtexts, however, are less obvious and are inadequately addressed. This element of tree planting and its discourse are explored in the following chapter on the work of the National Arbor Day Foundation.

THREE

The National Arbor Day Foundation

MODIFYING THE NATURAL WORLD

From cities, towns and byways shorn of the majestic,
uplifting beauty that only trees can provide, to the
barren desolation of dustbowls in place of productive
croplands, the prospects of a nation poor in trees is
simply too grim to contemplate.

National Arbor Day Foundation membership letter, 2000

The National Arbor Day Foundation was created to both commemorate and capitalize on the centenary of J. Sterling Morton's holiday for trees. The foundation, which has grown tremendously since its inception, reflects what characterized Morton himself: a love of trees, a gift for promotion, a belief in the human ability to transform the landscape, and a vision of the citizen as steward. Where Morton was an avowed politician, however, the National Arbor Day Foundation is political in less direct—though still powerful—ways. Though the National Arbor Day Foundation has never defined itself as a political organization, its environmental work, in line with David Harvey's contention that any engagement with the environment has social ramifications, is political by definition.

What is intriguing about the National Arbor Day Foundation as a political organization is that it seeks to hew to the middle ground, casting itself as apolitical—a safe harbor for those who want to shape the environment without making a political declaration. However, the foundation's work, in terms of its public materials, its organizational efforts, and its staff orientation, weaves a path around the apolitical middle, demonstrating leanings toward both sides of the environmental spectrum. The claim of neutrality is thus juxtaposed with a more complex reality in which the National Arbor Day Foundation both takes political positions and is available to others for use as a signifier of neutrality. The claim to apolitical status makes the foundation seem an appealing mechanism for individuals who see value in the image of the middle ground, the space where those who benefit most from hegemony capitalize on the opportunity to enlist support, or at least dampen resistance, across the political spectrum.

RE-CREATING A CAUSE

The National Arbor Day Foundation, even more than Arbor Day itself, is associated with one man's vision. The idea for the foundation came from another Nebraskan interested in promoting the welfare of his state and the environment. John Rosenow, the organization's founder, quit his job at the Nebraska Bureau of Tourism in order to generate enthusiasm for the Arbor Day holiday. Rosenow was only twenty-one years old at the time and admits to having had no grand vision for what the organization might become and what its place in the environmental firmament would be.[1]

In 1971, its first year of activity, the foundation was a nascent operation, more of a concept in fact, and its primary purpose was to raise awareness about the holiday and about trees. The foundation accomplished this by awarding prizes and generating public recognition for individuals and groups engaged in laudable tree planting activities. In its first ten years, the organization served as a clearinghouse for information: it sought out tree planting activities, brought them to the attention of the media, and provided technical advice to those interested in sponsoring such occasions.

THE FOUNDATION BRANCHES OUT

Begun as an organization that recognized the efforts of others, the National Arbor Day Foundation became a facilitator of members' planting activities and then grew into a collage of programs designed to provide a range of options for conservation activity. The foundation has a number of constituencies for its programs, including individual members, educators, professional or trade groups, farmers, local governments, national policy makers, and corporations. Its programs sustain its twin goals: to provide useful service, and to build the organization's influence and strengthen its base of support. A detailed survey of all of its programs would be superfluous, but the key programs merit examination, as they provide conduits for the foundation's message and meld its constituents into a coalition to pursue the foundation's agenda.

Tree City USA

Since its inception in the bicentennial year, 1976, Tree City USA has become one of the National Arbor Day Foundation's most successful programs and constitutes its most enduring link with the public. The link is indirect, however: the target of the program is municipal forestry staffs throughout the United States. The program was created and operates in conjunction with the U.S. Forest Service and the National Association of State Foresters (the latter funded in part by the former) and is cosponsored by the U.S. Conference of Mayors and the National League of Cities. The goal of Tree City USA is to foster not only the planting of trees in urban areas but also the development of programs that promote tree planting and ensure maintenance of the trees in perpetuity.

The National Arbor Day Foundation and the National Association of State Foresters have established four criteria that must be satisfied for a community to qualify for (or be awarded, in the lexicon of the program) Tree City USA status. First, the community must create and maintain a municipal, or in some cases voluntary, department responsible for urban forestry. The department's staff must include a professional forester or arborist; the National Arbor Day Foundation encourages the formal and informal participation of community members as well. Second, the community's city code must include a legal tree ordinance; models for drafting such ordinances are provided by the foundation. Such ordinances govern care and maintenance of the urban forest, regulate the removal of trees, and make trees a recognized component of the urban infrastructure. Third, at least two dollars per capita must be dedicated to the community's forestry program. Fourth, the community must proclaim and sponsor an official Arbor Day celebration.

When these conditions have been met, the community can promote its Tree City USA status. (This status is revoked if the community does not maintain the necessary conditions.) The foundation lists dividends—beyond the tangible healthy urban forest itself—that come with that status: citizen pride, public image, and financial assistance, among others. The descriptions of these benefits range from the emotional well-being of community members to the economic return that flows from having a green image. To facilitate widespread recognition of the Tree City USA communities, the foundation provides road signs to be posted at the entrances to the city, banners and flags, public recognition ceremonies, explanatory literature for distribution, and a range of public service announcements for media use. The Tree City USA program currently has more than twenty-six hundred towns and cities enrolled, and National Arbor Day Foundation material notes that more than 80 million Americans live in those communities.[2]

Trees for America

As noted above, the primary direct outreach effort of the National Arbor Day Foundation is its Trees for America program, which offers, in exchange for its basic membership fee, ten trees. Membership also includes periodic newsletters, a guide to trees with tips on planting and care, and discounts on the purchase of additional trees from the foundation. In recent years, members have been provided with a variety of tree types to choose from, an expansion on the earlier provision of only Colorado blue spruce. Now the choice includes the spruce, eastern red cedar, flowering dogwood, goldenrain tree, flowering crabapple, Washington hawthorn, and American redbud.

The trees are sent to members through the mail and are timed to correspond with appropriate planting periods for the respective hardiness zones of the country. To keep costs down and ensure the trees' viability, they are sent as dormant bare-root seedlings or saplings sealed within plastic, measuring between six and twelve inches in length. Each scrawny specimen is years away from becoming the robust tree that the foundation guarantees will grow from such humble beginnings (or will be replaced free). Indeed, the planting instructions direct members to cultivate their trees in a protected spot for a year before transplanting them to their permanent location. Over the years, critics have questioned the viability and suitability of the trees provided by the foundation, but increasing sophistication in the cultivation and choice of trees is being applied to the challenge of ensuring that trees mailed to members can thrive.

The number of trees provided annually in exchange for membership fees has remained fixed at ten for the duration of the program, but as the foundation has grown, the overall quantity of trees provided by Trees for America has grown too. The first year that the foundation had a membership was 1983, and the first membership figure, for 1984, was 203,784. Membership peaked in 1990 at 1,111,162, and for the year 2000 stood at 988,353.[3] Inasmuch as the primary function of the foundation is to promote tree planting, the number of trees and the size of the membership might be seen as a measure of the organization's success. Yet with a broader conservation goal in its agenda, and the growth of the organization as a significant interest, the basic membership fee—and the difficulty of maintaining member interest over the long-term—leaves the National Arbor Day Foundation pursuing a greater financial commitment from members. Tree planting is a start for conservation work, and the foundation does much to encourage it, but the organization's challenge is to maintain and increase members' level of activity.

Teach Youth about Trees

The foundation has a host of materials designed for classroom instruction in conjunction with and independent of Arbor Day celebrations. Teachers can chose from organized kits complete with curricular guides and individual items, including videos, informative posters, pamphlets and handout sheets, games, tree identification kits, and seeds for planting. Other articles available for pupils include stickers, rulers, and related items for use in and around the classroom that carry the National Arbor Day Foundation logo and a tree slogan. On-line material and other programs are also available to children, including a summer camp and an annual national poster contest for fifth grade pupils.

The curricula of the National Arbor Day Foundation's youth programs are designed to provide a broad knowledge of trees and to inspire tree planting and care. Their tone is scientific, and the language encourages participants to feel empowered with respect to the natural environment. One phrase that appears regularly in this material is "wise environmental stewardship," about which more will be said below. The foundation puts great stock in its educational activities, and the result is the high quality of the material, the range and amount available, and the material's widespread popularity and recognition. The Grow Your Own Tree kit, for example, has been honored by *Learning Magazine* as a Teacher's Choice Award winner. The foundation's national poster contest has grown each year, offering a different theme each time, and it now reaches nearly 1 million children annually.

THE FOUNDATION'S MESSAGES

Beyond its obvious slogan "Plant Trees," the organization communicates a number of themes through its material, some of them readily evident, others more subtle. As noted above, two clear purposes of the communication are to promote the foundation's work and to maintain its viability, and growth, as an organization. To these ends, the foundation positions itself as a service organization that helps the individual and society meet the challenges inherent in managing the environment. One of its key efforts, therefore, is to make those challenges known. Once the specific problem has been established, the solution proffered is, in the narrow sense and more broadly, to harness nature for specific goals. Reaching those goals is depicted as being among the benefits of tree planting, and the benefits are coupled with particular aspects of the challenges, so that the foundation offers a range of pairings—problems and solutions— neatly packaged for the consumer-member and the general public.

Defending against Nature

The challenge as depicted by the National Arbor Day Foundation is to plant enough trees to defuse the threats inherent in both natural and human-made environmental conditions. One striking feature of the foundation's material is that nature is portrayed as both something we need to defend and something we need to defend against. The latter is perhaps unanticipated in a conservation organization, yet is a clearly articulated component of the call to plant trees.[4]

Particularly in relation to the Conservation Trees program, primarily aimed at farmers and ranchers, nature is presented as a destructive force. In a letter to foundation members, President Rosenow reminds readers that their contribution will help plant trees that "act as critical barriers to the dry summer winds that can blow away precious farmland[,] . . . trees that fight water erosion." Having provided a foretaste of the problem, Rosenow then discusses the challenge faced by dustbowl farmers in the 1930s and warns, "THE WINDS STILL BLOW . . . THE RAIN STILL FALLS."[5] The warning gets even more emphatic as it makes a specific charge:

> Unless we plant more protective trees, the rains will cut gullies into our richest farmland, gorging and destroying an irreplaceable resource[,] . . . choking our streams and staining our rivers.
> The natural enemies of our land, the dry winds and the unchecked runoffs, will ravage ever more precious topsoil if you and I don't do our part to help plant conservation trees. In some places it is occurring today! In dry season you can see ominous dust clouds over America's farmland.[6]

Two images that often accompany this depiction of the threat to America's farms come in "before" and "after" versions titled "A World WITHOUT Trees" and "A World WITH Trees" (see figs. 5 and 6).[7] The images are in stark contrast to one another and offer a choice between

Figures 5 and 6. Images titled "A World WITHOUT Trees" and "A World WITH Trees" demonstrate the transformative effect of trees across a broad landscape. Reprinted with permission of the National Arbor Day Foundation.

Figures 7 and 8. The title for these two images, "Trees Make a World of Difference," poses an obvious choice for the urban landscape. Reprinted with permission of the National Arbor Day Foundation.

apocalypse and paradise. In the middle of the WITHOUT image is a community that looks exposed (it is described as "sun-baked" in its caption), isolated, and uninviting. In the WITH image is a bucolic and appealing community described as being composed of "shaded homes and streets." The countryside surrounding the town undergoes an even more graphic transformation from one image to the next, as does the river flowing through the landscape.

Text accompanying the images warns, "A world without trees would be a barren world. Giant dust storms would roll across the countryside, blowing away precious topsoil, choking people, plants, and animals. Parched fields could no longer grow enough food to feed the world's population. Hillsides would erode away, choking streams and rivers with silt."[8] The words and drawings strongly suggest the power of trees, and implicitly tree planting, and represent the triumph over nature. There is a human role in generating the harsh conditions of the "before" depiction, but more powerful is the sense of what can be accomplished "against" predatory nature. A separate set of images depict a city as a windy, treeless, harsh environment, with people cowering before the wind and shading their eyes from harsh light, as opposed to a tree-lined city that looks inviting and shady (though, curiously, it is devoid of people; see figs. 7 and 8).

Working with Nature

The sense of empowerment with respect to nature comes across in other National Arbor Day Foundation programs: empowerment comes with aiding nature rather than opposing it. The dominant message of the foundation's programs is that one should conserve and protect resources for future generations, though what constitutes conservation and protection encompasses a range of opinions. Conservation is cast as an act of improvement, however, granting agency through tree planting to those who seek to improve a nature impoverished by humans. A National Arbor Day Foundation member survey poses the question "Do you agree or disagree with this statement: 'Trees can make a significant difference in improving the environment'?"[9] Though *environment* is never defined, the list of improvements offered by the foundation, which accompanies the survey, is extensive and is regularly revisited in all the foundation's programs and publications. The benefits are linked, often explicitly, with particular problems that mark a treeless place, maintaining the pattern of problem and solution.

According to one membership solicitation, *"America desperately needs more trees — now!"* The reason offered is that "trees remove carbon dioxide from the air and produce the oxygen that we breathe," thus tree planting can play a vital role in "reversing the 'greenhouse effect,' and the heat and drought that result."[10] This calamity is one that the tree planter "can personally help avoid,"[11] and it occurs at both a national and a global scale. The foundation notes that *"millions of acres are being destroyed worldwide. And only an informed and aroused citizenry can counteract this dangerous practice through the care and planting of trees!"*[12]

More localized elements of tree planting, rather than the issue of global warming, have been the traditional fodder for National Arbor Day Foundation promotions, however. Many of these issues relate to the immediate environs of the members, ranging from the individual home plot to the street, neighborhood, community, and beyond. Cast as beneficial in a variety of ways, trees are characterized as contributing to the immediate welfare of the individual in economic, aesthetic, and health terms. The list of benefits that I alluded to earlier is deployed in relation to this localized environmental management, and many of the improvements said to result from this management are aimed at specific problems in direct or indirect ways: "The trees we plant . . . soon stretch up toward the sun giving shelter, shade, comfort, joy, beauty, and relief from the concrete jungle. They trap dust, diminish smog, reduce traffic noise. They produce oxygen and moderate the temperature. They provide a home for wildlife."[13]

In many cases the benefits are also coupled with an economic incentive for the tree planter and home or business owner. A National Arbor Day Foundation newsletter reports a study by the Environmental Protection Agency on the effect of urban heat islands and the role that trees can play in reducing their effect. It notes further that "planting a tree today may well mean dollars in your pocket tomorrow. A few well-placed trees will provide shade that can reduce summer air conditioning costs from 15 to 35 percent or more."[14] The value of the home itself will rise, according to the newsletter, though the precise amount is unclear, since the same page cites figures of 6–7 percent, "as much as twenty percent," and 10 percent (this last credited to the U.S. Forest Service).[15]

Other foundation materials point out the benefits that accrue to business districts which invest in beautification through tree planting. They cite studies from San Jose State University Department of Geography and the University of Washington showing that increased tree cover leads to increased profits.[16] Less direct gains are also reported, such as the power of a tree to generate, over a fifty-year span, $31,250 worth of oxygen and $62,000 worth of air pollution control, and to recycle $37,500 worth of water.[17]

Beyond the economic gains, there are less tangible contributions that come with tree planting. The foundation newsletter quotes Lester Brown of the Worldwatch Institute, who says, "Tree planting fosters community spirit and pride, bringing people together for a meaningful purpose that can build bridges and promote understanding," a sentiment that resonates with the long-established language of Arbor Day.[18] The newsletter goes on to cast the benefits of trees in terms of health, saying that "visual exposure to settings with trees has produced significant recovery from stress within five minutes, as indicated by changes in blood pressure and muscle tension."[19]

One other mechanism for communicating the benefits of trees, and the most far-reaching, albeit superficial, of the foundation's outreach tools, is its public service announcements. Each year, it sends a compact disc with a number of messages to each radio and television station in the United States. The public service announcements range from ten to sixty seconds in length and feature various music styles, including rock, country, contemporary, and "original," formatted for both radio and television. The text and images (for television) depict people of different ages and ethnic groups planting trees and engaging in celebratory occasions while explaining the reasons for and benefits of the planting.

In order to boost the announcements' effect and add to their appeal, a number of celebrities have been enlisted to act as spokesmen for the foundation. John Denver wrote and sang jingles for the National Arbor Day Foundation, and they have remained a part of the campaign since his death. The actor Eddie Albert, a longtime member of the foundation's board, lent his voice as well to the promotional material. A recent tactic employed by the foundation has been to place public service announcements before motion pictures, with the lead actor introducing the organization and its work and encouraging the viewer to get involved. Among those participating in this form of promotion have been the actors John Travolta and Tim Allen.

In all programs and message formats produced by the National Arbor Day Foundation, the constant theme is the need to plant trees, and to plant them for specific reasons. These reasons include a range of benefits that accrue to both people and nature, and they are cast in terms of improving the existing situation. As such, the foundation is portrayed as an environmental advocate, and there are repeated suggestions that "wise stewardship" and "wise environmental management" are essential for the welfare of the planet and our species. Indeed, the foundation is somewhat evangelical in this regard, seeking to gain, sustain, and inspire converts to the cause through its outreach. To further that goal, the foundation seeks partners for its work.

PARTNERS IN PLANTING

Despite the growth of the National Arbor Day Foundation since its inception, it remains a relatively small organization, and much of its practical work, particularly growing, planting, and caring for trees, is carried out by proxies, partners, and foundation members. Chief among these are the city and state foresters who participate in the Tree City USA program. Coordination of joint efforts often is generated through the interface between the foundation and the National Association of State Foresters. Funding for the cooperation comes, in part, from the U.S. Forest Service's Cooperative Forestry program, discussed in chapter 5. Other funding for the foundation's programs comes from grants offered by local, state, and federal agencies.

In this regard, the government provides a significant boost to the foundation's activities, and for 1998, the last year for which figures are available, such grants totaled $662,790 out of the total revenue of $6,544,190.[20] The foundation reports that more than half a billion dollars was allocated by governments through Tree City USA programs in 1997–1998, but the true value of the government's role in foundation activities is impossible to quantify. The hours invested by foresters, and the promotion of the National Arbor Day Foundation through Tree City USA and Arbor Day celebrations and the like, go far beyond the direct monetary investment.[21] Manifestations of government support for the foundation crop up in unexpected places as well, such as a four-page display of tree planting methods and National Arbor Day Foundation membership information in the navy's *All Hands* magazine—so far as I know, there are no trees planted on ships, though military bases can now qualify for Tree City USA status.[22] Even more curious was Oakridge National Labs' response to my query about their biomass generation programs. Along with a brochure about their activities, the mailing included a pamphlet from the California Poplar Council and a paper copy of the National Arbor Day Foundation home page on the Web.[23] From tax-exempt status to direct contributions of funds and the labor of government employees, there is a true partnership between the government and the foundation in terms of planting trees and promoting the message of Arbor Day.

The foundation finds partnerships in the corporate sector as well and, in fact, has been pursuing such relationships more aggressively in recent years. The level of corporate support currently represents around 20 percent of the foundation's revenue, a sevenfold increase from 1995 to 2000.[24] The biggest corporate supporter is the Keebler Corporation, whose product packaging shows cookie-baking elves working out of a tree. To promote the tree planting agenda and its own profits, Keebler subsidizes the foundation's annual fifth grade student poster contest, which puts the company's advertising campaign in classrooms throughout the country. And cookie packages have carried a mail-in coupon for National Arbor Day Foundation membership, asking children and their parents to enclose a number of product labels with their regular membership fee.

Though Keebler is the biggest corporate partner, over one hundred others furnish various kinds and levels of support. Some sponsor tree planting activities among their own employees, others simply donate money, and still others link their concepts or services to the foundation to mutual advantage. Wal-Mart, for instance, places the foundation's promotional material in its store circulars during the annual National Arbor Day week, providing access to approximately 10 million consumers. Triangle Pacific, a hardwood flooring manufacturer, has partnered with the National Arbor Day Foundation in the interest of "giving something back" to the environment that supplies the company's raw material.

Other supporters have no particular business connection to trees or the environment but want to be associated with the cause. This list consists of financial institutions, high-tech companies, food service corporations, and many others, including a small number of timber, tobacco, and alcohol manufacturers. When partnering, the foundation usually seeks out logical associations, such as the one suggested by Keebler's tree motif or the manufacture of wood products, but they are not averse to partners such as Toyota, one of their newer alliances. Donations range from minuscule to many thousands of dollars, and each one secures the company's right to publicize its association with the foundation, though not all donors avail themselves of this opportunity. The association is reciprocal, of course, and the support of the many corporations, the government, and a million individual members gives the foundation a powerful seal of approval that it, too, can boast.

CLAIMING THE MIDDLE GROUND

The fundamental message of the National Arbor Day Foundation is wholesome and simple. Planting trees does bestow many of the benefits articulated by the organization and other planters, and millions of people have planted trees that provide shade, beauty, and more. At the same time, the language of its programs and publicity is complex and has embedded in it powerful statements about relations between humans and the environment and about the meaning of stewardship. Despite the inherently political character of the environmental sphere, or rather, because of it, foundation staff members eschew any declarations or admissions of a political element to their work.

It is important to question the role of an individual or institution in contributing to a hegemonic conception, and to attempt to assess the degree to which such participation is deliberate or unconscious. It is often difficult, however, to get people to situate their work or attitudes within deep political currents and philosophical orientations, especially when they claim to be politically neutral. A claim of neutrality can, in fact, be taken at face value and yet still be obviously incorrect. The leadership of the National Arbor Day Foundation may aim for neutrality and perhaps be oblivious of its own place in the broader political context that Gramsci or Harvey have analyzed. To determine whether this is the case, I pursued two avenues of examination in my interviews with staff members. First, I asked if the work of the foundation was political or could be construed as political. Second, and related, I probed the foundation's alliances and partnerships and looked at whether those partners, or nonpartners, might use the foundation's work in a political manner.[25]

Along with the fundamental mission of the foundation, staffers repeatedly emphasize the political neutrality of their work.[26] At times this takes the form of "something for everyone" declarations, but at other times there is a clear effort to distance the foundation from parties or causes identified as belonging to what they characterize as the realm of politics. Staffers say that they ignore the raging debates about environmental issues, preferring instead to devote their attention to ways to further their work. It is not that the foundation condemns those with a more overt environmental role, or those who are less green, for such judgment could constitute a political position. Rather, it maintains a live-and-let-live attitude toward those who share the views of the foundation as well as those who do not. Those of like mind, even organizations that compete with the National Arbor Day Foundation for scarce resources, are wished well and discussed with admiration, while those with whom the foundation differs in philosophical orientation are seen as candidates for education about trees and environmental stewardship.

The foundation sees its ability to remain neutral as an important asset, and staffers insist that their work is not "controversial" in any way. In fact, Rosenow suggests that "we all" agree on tree planting, and that planting trees, an almost instinctual drive, brings out people's sense of capability. The foundation's role, therefore, is simply to facilitate and support that which is inherent in our emotional constitution: the work is a natural expression of powerful inclinations.

PROMOTING THE POWER OF PEOPLE AND TREES

One of the National Arbor Day Foundation's messages, as part of its call to plant trees, is that tree planting elevates those who plant, no matter who they may be, no matter what broader agenda they may pursue. Moreover, just as the foundation guarantees trees that will grow, it offers the benefits of planting in a manner that makes them seem guaranteed too: if you plant a tree, a whole list of good things will happen. While the programs and materials speak of and promote trees as the tool for action, and certainly as things of inherent beauty and worth, it is the agency of the individual that puts the process in motion.

The result is that the organization offers something for everyone, both individuals and communities of all sizes. Tree planting enriches the individual in intangible ways, such as by enhancing one's moral fiber and citizenship (see fig. 9), and by supplying financial rewards, such as an increase in property value or a reduction in energy costs. As for the foundation's commercial partners, their corporate officers and employees are improved as individuals, and the corporate properties on which trees are planted benefit too. The primary emphasis of the foundation is on the immediate: trees should be planted to benefit the here and now of the planter.

In two areas, the foundation reaches beyond the United States, and in them its programs and policies are most obviously political. The first is global warming. Many of the organization's individual programs pinpoint global warming as one environmental problem that requires action, and the reduction of global warming as one benefit of these programs. According to the foundation's formula, trees = carbon sequestration.

Figure 9. The foundation's national tree election appeals in both image and sentiment to nationalism, and associates patriotism with its lessons of citizenship. Reprinted with permission of the National Arbor Day Foundation.

Although the link between anthropogenic greenhouse gas emissions and global warming is increasingly accepted as truth, the foundation did not wait until that debate was finally resolved before joining in the effort to reduce global warming.

The second area in which the foundation extends itself is in its Rain Forest Rescue program. In part, this program is linked to climate issues, as the foundation points out that "the uncontrolled burning of the rain forest is pouring out carbon dioxide faster than surrounding forests can cleanse it from the air. The result: burning rain forest is a major contributor to the greenhouse effect now predicted by many scientists."[27] Rain Forest Rescue departs from the organization's typical programs in that it does not involve planting trees. Instead, a member can choose to dedicate the ten-dollar annual donation to preserving "2500 sq feet or more" of tropical rain forest. An adjunct of this program is the Rain Forest Rescue Premium Coffee offer, which is purchased separately from foundation membership. The coffee, shade grown in the El Triunfo Biosphere Reserve, is bought via monthly subscription. The benefits, beyond the beverage itself, are the preservation of the rain forest and migratory songbird habitat, resulting in more songbirds in subscribers' neighborhoods.

With these two elements of extended reach, the foundation offers the power to engage, and manage, the environment at the global scale. Though there is no shortage of controversy surrounding climate change and tropical rain forests, Rosenow and his staff insist that the work of these programs is not political, and they offer no judgment of anyone who may contribute to the problems in question. Thus, according to the foundation's staff, there is no inherent contradiction in accepting support from U.S. and multinational corporations commonly associated with carbon accumulation in the atmosphere and the destruction of the rain forest. In fact, the participation of such companies is seen as a sign that the foundation's approach of education and outreach is a success. Perhaps at some level this is true. It is also possible, of course, that the foundation is being cynically, or just practically, used by corporations as an emblem of environmental responsibility. When I posed this possibility, it was unanimously downplayed. Later, Rosenow acknowledged that, while some sponsors might in fact be opportunistic, their sponsorship still made it possible to get trees planted and to influence the people planting them. Trees, it seems, have influence even in the court of capitalism, just as they do in the backyards of the masses.

SITUATING THE FOUNDATION

John Rosenow emphasizes that there is no such thing as a private tree: every tree benefits people in addition to the one who planted it. At the same time, the National Arbor Day Foundation is geared toward individual participation: it wants people to learn about trees, to see them, touch them, plant them. It views conservation as an interactive process, and its message promotes proactive environmental stewardship. Though it eschews the term *wise use* for political reasons, the phrase "wise environmental stewardship" and the characterization of trees as a renewable natural resource frequently appear in foundation material.

In some respects, the very lack of an articulated political agenda can be interpreted as a deliberate position, as the organization uses its voice only in "positive" ways, and not to criticize current practices or policies. In this regard, silence can be a powerful message, and one that finds support and appreciation among those with a vested interest in the status quo. What makes the foundation such an attractive ally in this regard is that it reaches out to individuals in a very direct way. It literally puts trees in the hands of millions of people, enlisting them in a relationship with nature that it defines in its material, and in partnerships with other supporters that are not so obvious, yet powerful nonetheless. Although its classroom curricula introduce children to environmentalists like John Muir and Rachel Carson, in the material directed to adults those voices, and indeed any protests, are absent.[28] Ever since the first Arbor Day in 1872, the message has been repeated with fervor: plant trees—change the world. From the perspective of the National Arbor Day Foundation, it seems that the world need not be changed much.

FOUR

American Forests

PLANTING THE FUTURE

You don't survive in this town by being partisan.

Deborah Gangloff,
American Forests

In 1972, the National Arbor Day Foundation celebrated the centennial of Arbor Day, and American Forests launched a new tree planting program. At the time, American Forests was approaching its own centennial and was, in many respects, a moribund organization suffering from low membership and a lack of clear purpose. That year, at its National Tree Planting Conference held in New Orleans, American Forests announced the new Trees for America (soon changed to Tree Time USA) program, designed to motivate the public and generate support for the organization across "the widest possible cross section of people, interests and organizations."[1]

Tree Time USA was intended to be a decade-long project for American Forests, and the plan included rejuvenating Arbor Day, working with state foresters to develop programs at the state and municipal level, advocating legislation to support tree planting, developing educational materials for schools, reaching out to youth groups, broadcasting public service announcements, and many other such activities.[2] A remarkably similar agenda won for the National Arbor Day Foundation a membership base of a million people, while American Forests spent the subsequent twenty years maintaining a tenuous hold on survival while failing to implement a cogent set of programs to capture and mobilize public support.

Ultimately, however, its Global ReLeaf tree planting program rescued American Forests as an organization, giving it a broader constituency and increased revenue. This chapter explores the transition of American Forests from a policy and technical forestry organization concerned with growing and administering forests to a popular citizens group. It examines the image presented in its journal, *American Forests*, and in membership and promotional materials produced for public consumption, as well as the internal deliberations that accompanied the changes marked by the growth of the Global ReLeaf program.

The rapid and widespread success of Global ReLeaf, explored against the background of the relative failure of traditional American Forests programs, highlights the appeal of tree planting and the way the organization chose to capitalize on the popularity of this activity. In order to promote its work, American Forests taps into the history of trees, accentuates their roles in nature, associates different cultural figures with trees, and then positions itself as the chief advocate of this powerful natural asset. The organization then makes this package of meanings and power available to those who advance its goals, whether they are individuals making small contributions or corporations providing major financial support. At the same time, American Forests directs explicit attention to the profit that corporations can draw from their association with Global ReLeaf, demonstrating the power of an association with trees via sponsorship of a group that facilitates coalitions along the environmental spectrum. By softening environmental dispute in this way, American Forests performs the function of civil society highlighted by Gramsci: it constructs a bridge between capital interests and the general public, providing a ground on which they can meet as partners.

With the success of Global ReLeaf, new partnerships were formed that molded government experts, individual supporters, and wealthy corporations into highly touted coalitions. According to American Forests' modest claims, these individuals and groups are involved in improving their environment; the organization's more bombastic claims assert that they are saving the world. By enlisting its members and the general public in such efforts, and more broadly, by promoting its work and the agency of its partners as vehicles for relieving the globe, the organization generates a share of the discourse on tree planting.

Moreover, by accepting the sponsorship of major oil, coal, and timber companies and producers of almost any consumer product from automobiles to picture frames, the organization makes the Global ReLeaf seal of approval available to anyone seeking to benefit from association with the hegemonic discourse of the environment. In creating an allegedly neutral space where participants can meet and cooperate in a win-win agenda, the organization both accredits and apportions the power to control nature and manage the environment. Though American Forests periodically nods in the direction of fundamental environmental principles, the main premise of Global ReLeaf is that damage can be undone by planting trees. A secondary but critical premise is that those doing the most damage are also doing the most planting. Capital interests gain from this discourse of trees and the organization's seal of approval, and the public is invited to participate in an effort—one that purportedly transforms the environment—whose proud sponsors are the very industries that form the focus of environmental concern.

For many of the corporations associated with Global ReLeaf, profit is one, if not the primary, motivation in supporting the program—an aspect of the relationship that does not trouble American Forests. Obscuring motive and focusing disproportionately on the benefits of planting is one function of the Global ReLeaf material, and the role the program has in driving, defining, and funding American Forests as an organization reveals the versatility of tree planting as simultaneously a popular and "innocent"—indeed productive—engagement with the environment and an overt tool of corporate America. One implicit message to environmentalists from the Global ReLeaf program is, if you can't beat 'em, plant with 'em. The discourse of trees, while detailing the symptoms of environmental damage, remains vague about the causes.

CREATING A BANDWAGON

In order to understand Global ReLeaf in context, it is necessary to go back and examine Tree Time USA and the period preceding American Forests' current momentum. At that time, the organization asked its membership and the broader public, "Can America plant enough trees in the next decade to meet the environmental and forest products needs of a growing population?" and it answered, "Of course it can. And it will."[3]

With Tree Time USA, American Forests was not actually getting into the tree planting business, but rather was acting as a promoter and facilitator of partnerships and programs that would support planting. The policy of the organization was "to encourage state and federal governments, industry and private citizens to plant trees where they are needed, in cities, on the farms, or in the forests."[4] The premise was simple: "To plant a tree is to invest in a better future[,] and the person who plants a tree will not destroy the forest."[5] Though the organization wanted to support planting across the range of individuals and groups and locales, it was cautious about becoming associated with some who sought to join it in planting partnerships. The organization's leadership noted that it was important to "remain impartial and retain [the] conservation image," and that the organization "cannot approve or disapprove or endorse any particular company for its program."[6]

Despite this cautionary note, American Forests was interested in establishing coalitions and raising its profile, and its tree planting efforts were intended at least in part to generate membership for the organization. To the ongoing frustration of the staff and board of directors, membership did not increase and American Forests continued to struggle to maintain its membership base and financial viability. Discussions over the years touched on the role of the journal in appealing to the public, the policy positions taken by the organization, the outreach efforts designed to enlist newcomers and sustain long-term supporters, and why all these efforts were failing.

In the post–Earth Day era, the organization hoped that enthusiasm for the environment generally, and tree planting in particular, would translate into support for the organization. Yet with its membership base both aging and shrinking, it was clear that the group needed new directions and tactics to recapture relevancy and ensure its own sustainability. Until the late 1980s, this sent the organization in pursuit of various constituencies and produced a nonconfrontational approach to issues that provoked a range of positions in environmental debates. As one critic on the board phrased it, the organization was "for everything and against nothing." The journal was denounced as being "trite, dull, and obsolescent."[7]

Though in the past American Forests had taken clear positions on various issues related to forests and natural resources, the lack of a stable and sizeable constituency—in the form of paying members—was an old story for this organization. Thus the loss of focus was only one problem identified by board members, and one that lacked an obvious remedy. Given that previously members were mainly timber industry affiliates or owners of small woodlots, and given the new, burgeoning appeal of forms of environmentalism, continued lobbying in Washington on forest policy issues was not an obvious panacea for American Forests' ills, because it lacked appeal and a role for new members. Divergent positions on the organization's board complicated the search for a significant role and message. Even the cautious positions on environmental issues that American Forests did take elicited concern from those with a stake in timber industry policies. The call for a reduction in atmospheric pollution, for instance, drew the following response from a board member (and future head of American Forests) who also served as vice president for the Westvaco timber company:

> [American Forests'] policy position on acid rain . . . is going to cause us some real problems. I'm already getting negative feedback from industry, including my own management, because the issue is so "hot" and so divisive within the industry. Also, and recognizing that this is especially sensitive in the Northeast, there is still strong skepticism about the *general* effect of acidic depositions on forests.
>   The problem is that [American Forests'] simple position appears too "environmental." Our real role should be to "broker the truth" in the broader issue of forest decline. It could sell a lot of memberships and subscriptions if we establish credibility as a reporter of all views,

theories and research—and an advocate in specific situations where the facts are solid.[8]

Corporate America was an ongoing source of financial support that American Forests hoped would continually grow larger; thus the alienation of donors, not least those from the timber industry, represented a potential cost to the organization that it could ill afford to bear. American Forests was actively seeking to enlist timber companies as supporters, and it offered each major forest company a free trial subscription to the journal and followed up with an invitation to join the organization.[9] This recruitment strategy was connected to broader policy issues, as shown in the organization's "Action Plan," drawn up by Executive Vice President Neil Sampson, which stated, "The 1985 goals include the continuation of the 1984 positioning of American Forests so that confidence in the organization among potential corporate members continues to increase. This does not mean turning American Forests into a voice for corporations, but rather turning it into a more effective voice for conservation; one that can be helpful when issues arise where only a credible conservation organization can effectively promote and win."[10]

The action plan also proposed establishing a biweekly newsletter for board members, state foresters, leaders of the National Association of State Foresters, U.S. Forest Service leaders, corporate executives who were members of American Forests, and what the plan called simply American Forests "activists."[11] The composition of this group reveals the traditional base of American Forests and demonstrates its restrictions in its role as a credible conservation organization. The group clearly was unable to take any position that would undermine support from a particular and powerful set of participants that was anything but neutral when it came to forest policy.[12] Yet despite marketing surveys, outreach to various sectors, and an effort to generate enthusiasm for trees and the organization, American Forests continued to progress toward bankruptcy and dissolution. Reflecting organizational ambivalence, one board critic caustically observed, "While the Reagan Administration has been making a conscious and successful effort to gut the 'balanced use' of our public lands[,] . . . we have been telling our readers how to grow 'Pecans for Profit.'"[13]

CASTING ABOUT FOR RELEVANCY

As the 1980s progressed and the fortunes of the organization continued their downward path, members proposed additional programs, reconsidered old approaches, and brought in new blood to stimulate the leadership. Yet the specific identity and purpose that would galvanize support for the organization remained elusive. An example of the ongoing string of nonstarters was the Friends of the National Forests program proposed in 1987. Conceived as a mechanism to generate and direct support for the Forest Service, its first step was to create a task force to study and comment on management practices in the national forests. The task force was drawn from American Forests' board of directors and included a retired chief of the U.S. Forest Service, the dean of a major university forestry program, a timber company executive, an oil company executive, and a private forester. The organization also prepared a lengthy brochure called *America's Forests*, which had the following objectives:

- Orient foreign nationals, especially visitors
- Provide background for students
- Reinforce "The American Way" of managing forests in a democracy
- Demonstrate how the various major forest ownerships contribute to America's forest wealth[14]

The Forest Service, the Weyerhaeuser Company, and other companies provided funding for the brochure, and the reviewers for the project—who were not members of the task force—were drawn from the pool of industry executives, federal and state foresters, and forestry school faculty members associated with American Forests and its work.[15]

Clearly the organization had yet to find its new direction and tone, but continued failure with the tried and true was an increasingly impractical option. Proposals for the future included addressing the destruction of tropical forests ("a big money raiser"), promotion of highway trees and greenways ("could endear us to a broad constituency"), and support for planting windbreaks and shelterbelts ("would gain us friends in many areas, and show up the Arbor Day Foundation's 'conservation trees' program for exactly what it is: a fund-raising hype that has no real program for actually doing something about increasing the number and value of 'conservation trees' used by private landowners").[16] Ultimately, none of these ideas was adopted as the vehicle for rehabilitating American Forests, though none was entirely discarded either. Instead, the introduction of global climate change, and particularly the issue of carbon dioxide, presented an opportunity for the organization to fashion itself as a phoenix and rise again.

CREATING GLOBAL RELEAF

Suddenly, in 1988, American Forests found its issue. The organization's vice president asked, *"Is it time or appropriate for AF to consider a major change in focus and constituency . . .* to provide leadership on THE important forest issue of this era as its founders did over a century ago?"[17] That issue, broadly cast, was that "forest pollution/greenhouse effect/worldwide deforestation and general lack of good forest management[,] or however we characterize it, is [collectively] a massive subject of extreme importance to the human race as well as to trees and forests."[18] Specifically, the issue concerned the effects of increasing atmospheric carbon dioxide, the associated global warming, and the potential to offset those effects through "global reforestation."

An early working document for a program to address the issue proposed "ReLeaf for Global Warming: A National Citizen's Action Campaign." The stated objective was to "mobilize the American public to take actions to improve their environment, reduce the buildup of carbon dioxide in the atmosphere, and address global warming as a serious public policy issue." Among the goals was to "create, publicize and report progress on a national citizen's campaign to plant 50 million new trees in energy-conserving locations in the United States by 1992."[19] The program was to be launched in the fall of 1988, with a media blitz including op-ed pieces, public service announcements, and advertisements, along with direct mail fund-raising and outreach and the creation of new literature to promote the program and the organization.

The speed with which the staff of American Forests shifted its emphasis and resources to the new program and the message it carried created a sense of unease for some board members. The past president Perry Hagenstein expressed a number of concerns that he and others shared, among them that "in the rush to 'beat the competition' with a PR campaign[,] . . . we will have a product that is poorly developed. The arguments for rushing ahead sound like those for the Plant America's Trees program, which folded quickly."[20] Also at issue was whether Global ReLeaf was nothing more than "a window of opportunity for American Forests to capture attention and a focus only until a cool summer causes public interest to fade," a policy adopted "just to fatten [the] pocketbook."[21] Concerns of a substantive rather than programmatic nature were raised as well, with one board member relating donor sentiment that suggested the organization was "on controversial grounds scientifically with our Global ReLeaf program—that sufficient areas for planting on a scale to affect global warming are not available in the United States."[22]

THE SPREAD OF GLOBAL RELEAF

Though conceived as a program by and for all Americans, Global ReLeaf was also part of the effort to boost the financial health of American Forests. Thus, in addition to delivering a message and planting trees, generating revenue was an important consideration. By 1989, potential supporters were being approached with an appeal that related to the Global ReLeaf program and to the mutual benefit that could be found through industry-organization partnerships. In a letter to a timber company owner, American Forests executive director Neil Sampson listed some of the companies that had already established a relationship with the organization, including the Amway Corporation, the winery of Ernest and Julio Gallo (which donated $250,000), Safeway Stores (which printed 13 million grocery bags with Global ReLeaf information and a mail-in coupon), and the Rust-Oleum Corporation (which promised a fifty-cent donation from the sale of every can of their product). Sampson went on to note in this letter, "Company after company is coming to us to enter into Global ReLeaf partnerships—but *not one forest products company!!!*"[23]

In the early years of Global ReLeaf, public policy was seen as a significant component of the program and one that could incorporate the interests of the timber industry. American Forests sought to champion the industry on both private and public lands and at different scales. A short list of goals for rural forests included the following planks:

- Each state should have a working program that assures adequate reforestation of any land where timber harvest[s] are conducted, unless land use changes are involved. Federal tax law should continue to provide reforestation tax incentive.

- The 1990 Farm Bill should contain incentives for reforesting an additional 20 million acres of marginal crop and pasture lands through extension and expansion of the Conservation Reserve. It should also contain new incentives for establishing windbreaks, shelterbelts and st[r]eam corridor forests.

- Federal and State programs that provide education, technical, and financial assistance to nonindustrial private forest owners should be expanded, with a target of doubling their current effort by 1992.

- Forest managers should double the acreage of U.S. forests that are well-stocked and growing at their estimated potential rate of vigor by the turn of the century. On the federally-owned forests, the reforestation backlog should be eliminated.[24]

This set of policy pursuits would promote tree planting and, at the same time, dovetail with programs that would benefit the timber industry and provide it with various government subsidies for its activities. As a result, American Forests could pitch its policy work as being a part of the partnership with industry, and Global ReLeaf as a program that would provide universal benefit. In an era in which forest issues were increasingly becoming contentious, the organization sought to position Global ReLeaf as a win-win situation for all its constituencies and supporters. In a message to the executive committee, Sampson noted:

The Global ReLeaf message is that healthy forests help stabilize global environmental systems, the most symptomatic of which is climate.

American Forests' campaign will reach a wide, and somewhat alarmed[,]
American public, with the idea that healthy forests everywhere . . . are a
vital part of a healthy world. Secondary message: trees that grow fastest
[generally those planted by and for commercial forestry] are best for
helping stabilize [the] climate and environment.[25]

As Global ReLeaf moved the organization into the realm of mass
appeals, however, criticism from within came from both sides of the environmental spectrum. While some were concerned with the characterization of global challenges, others took a different tack. One board member
voiced her reservation, saying, "I am still extremely concerned about the
program and our organization being discredited if we continue to pursue
corporate sponsors who have a very strong incentive to make the public
think that planting trees is a more effective means of offsetting global
warming than is changing their behavior."[26] At the same time, pragmatists
spoke to the ongoing struggle to enlist aid from the sector served by
American Forests' policy orientation. One board member wrote, "Our
experience over the past two years raises serious questions about some
traditional constituencies. Our results suggest that American Forests
receives 'undying gratitude' from forest landowners, many sectors of federal, state, and local government that service various forest ownerships,
professional foresters, and so forth. American Forests does not receive
their financial support to the degree necessary to balance its budget."[27]

The organization thus faced the challenge of maintaining relations
with its traditional protimber allies while generating financial support
from new and additional interest groups, among them those who
opposed the protimber cadre. The expansion of Global ReLeaf took two
principal directions. One was a corporate outreach campaign unrelated
to the timber industry. Any business interested in partnering with
American Forests might support particular programs or the broader
goals of the organization. The second approach was aimed at the general
public, including readers of the organization's journal but also a far
broader pool of the "environmentally inclined" (see fig. 10). Ads in the
journal and elsewhere offered easy participation under the slogan "Plant
a tree, cool the globe." One issue of the newsletter assured readers,
"Every time you plant a tree, you're helping to solve what may be the

Figure 10. Patterned after an old-style fruit box label, one of the primary emblems of the Global ReLeaf program recalls the past while promising the future, generating an icon of a wholesome America. Reprinted with permission of American Forests.

greatest environmental problem of our lifetime, global warming," and asked them, "Won't you do your part to help cool the globe?"[28] In order to generate support for Global ReLeaf, the journal and a special newsletter were deployed to report the growing number of offshoots, or "daughter" projects, of the program and the details of its goals and implementation. To broaden Global ReLeaf's appeal, American Forests began to focus more on trees' functions in the environment and the role individuals can play in planting them, as evidenced by one of the organization's observations in its newsletter:

> Trees. It may sound like too simple a response to such a complex problem [global warming], but let's look at some facts: Trees remove CO_2 from the air and use it to produce wood and oxygen. Three trees

properly planted on the south and southwest sides of a building in the United States can reduce cooling costs by 10 to 50 percent. There are at least 100 million tree planting sites around homes and businesses in America's towns and cities. Planting those 100 million trees could offset carbon dioxide emissions by 33 million tons a year, saving Americans $44 billion in the process.[29]

CONSOLIDATING AROUND SUCCESS

In its first two years, Global ReLeaf was a promotional campaign that made education and public recognition its primary tools, a strategy similar to the one undertaken by the National Arbor Day Foundation during its first years. In 1990, however, American Forests created a new component of the program and called it "Global ReLeaf Forests." This aspect of Global ReLeaf was oriented toward planting, and it offered public participation on a "one tree for one dollar" basis. As early as 1991, Global ReLeaf was seen as a vehicle that could lead American Forests "into profitability by harnessing a good idea"; however, despite the growth of the program, the organization remained financially vulnerable.[30] As Global ReLeaf began to generate more localized or specialized "daughter" projects such as planting for specific events or memorials, voices within the organization continued to express reluctance to concentrate too narrowly on tree planting, which in the past had been an often marginal component of American Forests' agenda. Among the concerns of those who complained was that the National Arbor Day Foundation was already associated with tree planting, and that efforts to mimic or surpass it were unlikely to bring the quick relief that American Forests needed to survive.[31]

Still, organization officials persisted in their belief that Global ReLeaf was the ticket to success; they hoped to find, as Sampson put it, "new and better, more compelling ways to say, 'send us your $$ and we will . . .' Once we fill in that blank successfully, in a believable and compelling way, people will send $$."[32] One way to fill the blank was to offer many options under the Global ReLeaf umbrella, tailored both to particular planting needs and to particular donor interests. New projects carried names like Global ReLeaf Heritage Forests, Global ReLeaf Emergency Tree Fund, and Global ReLeaf International. ReLeaf projects were also created for and named after specific locations—for example, Fairfax ReLeaf in Virginia. ReLeaf projects were funded through sponsored events that had nothing to do with tree planting in and of themselves and through a host of other fund-raising mechanisms. By 1994, the list of corporate sponsors and the range of programs were already quite impressive. A partial list of supporters included Absolut Vodka, American Electric Power, Briggs and Stratton Corporation, *Business Week*, the Davey Tree Company, Gateway 2000, Reebok International, Scholastic Incorporated, and Texaco Corporation.[33]

In 1995, American Forests staffers stated:

> Global ReLeaf and its family of related programs are proven contributors in terms of membership (citizen involvement), income, and mission. It is also focused (plant trees) and simple. It needs to be elevated on the organizational chart to a position of parity with other program groups to be certain it gets the managerial attention it needs and deserves and to emphasize the huge tree planting and fundraising potential of this initiative.[34]

By 1996, American Forests had responded to these suggestions and replaced its executive director with the staff member that had been serving as vice president in charge of Global ReLeaf, the program that was becoming the flagship of the organization.

Deborah Gangloff, the new executive director, changed the name to Global ReLeaf 2000 in honor of the upcoming millennial turn. She reintroduced the program to readers and members in the first issue of *American Forests* after the transition of power. According to Gangloff, "Before Global ReLeaf, community tree groups were few and projects largely ceremonial. By awakening the corporate community to the value of trees, 340 projects have been supported by $2.8 million in grants through Global ReLeaf. *Partners, such as government agencies, corporations, and non-profits, are the heart and soul of the campaign.*"[35] Though corporations and government sponsors were certainly critical to the financial success of American Forests, Global ReLeaf sought new ways to enlist individuals in its cause as well.

In its journal, advertisements in other venues, and public service announcements in the media, the organization proposed six avenues for support of Global ReLeaf. The first was to plant a tree and send American Forests the details about what was planted, where, and when, so that the tree could be included in the tally of Global ReLeaf plantings. The second way was to call American Forests toll free and contribute ten dollars, which the organization would use to contract for the planting of ten trees on public lands undergoing restoration. The third way was to use the organization's Website, rather than the telephone, to donate money for tree planting contracts. The fourth was to contribute to another daughter program of Global ReLeaf, also by phone or Website. The fifth way, and one that has proven highly successful for the organization, was for supporters to purchase consumer goods from an American Forests partner; for each item purchased, the company would make a donation to Global ReLeaf. Furniture, flooring, clothing, cars—all could be acquired from companies that would then make a donation to the program. Finally, the opportunity to become a corporate sponsor was listed, along with the encouraging observation that "there are as many different ways to participate as there are kinds of companies" and the offer to customize a program to meet a donor company's particular needs.[36] Indeed, the growth of Global ReLeaf has been accompanied by a proliferation of local ReLeaf organizations funded by corporations; the core program has branched into various specialized niches. Individual projects are now dedicated to urban tree planting, international tree planting, targeted commemorative plantings, and so on. One of these projects had a part in the Tommy Hilfiger perfume promotion mentioned in chapter 1. American Forests provided the trees, and the toll-free hotline for Global ReLeaf appeared on the instructions that accompanied each of the "Global ReLeaf tree seedlings."[37]

THE LANGUAGE OF MODIFICATION AND IMPROVEMENT

In order to encourage its journal readers, and the general public, to take advantage of opportunities to support American Forests, Global ReLeaf had to convince them of the need to take action, why they should do it with trees, and why they should participate in this particular program. While carbon reduction was a central issue of the campaign from the outset, a host of other benefits from tree planting have been part of the suite of motivations offered for supporting Global ReLeaf. In fact, the program states that there are "a thousand-and-one reasons to plant a tree."[38] The reasons range from the altruistic to the mercenary, but most are included in "packages" of benefits—while targeting a specific purpose, one realized other dividends simultaneously. Thus, even those unconvinced that global warming is occurring, or simply unmotivated by such large-scale issues, can be enlisted in the tree-planting effort, something that was particularly important before global warming became commonly accepted as a "real" problem.

An examination of the list of benefits reveals a great deal of overlap between American Forests' reasons for planting and those articulated by the National Arbor Day Foundation. While the latter advocates and depicts radical transformation of the countryside and cityscape by way of trees, American Forests has a more ambitious agenda—as evidenced by the name Global ReLeaf—and its language offers efficacy to the individual at the global scale. Though Global ReLeaf does not adopt the problem/solution formula per se, it does suggest that a more perfect world can be had by planting trees, and at times offers to create that world (see fig. 11). Several approaches to the campaign warrant further examination.

THE NUMBERS GAME

One distinctive element of the Global ReLeaf campaign is a particular emphasis on the number of trees planted. Material distributed to American Forests members regularly boasts of the number of trees already planted by the program and uses this as an invitation and incentive for members to maintain or increase their level of support. American Forests also regularly reports both the number of trees planted through partnerships with corporate sponsors and the number planted to reha-

Plant the Future Today!

A Million Trees
for Earth Day
MARCH 1 - MAY 1, 2001

$\left\{\begin{array}{c}\text{EARTH DAY 2001} \\ \text{SUNDAY, APRIL 22}\end{array}\right\}$

JOIN THE CAMPAIGN

DOWNLOADS

TELL A FRIEND

COUNT YOUR TREES

LINKS AND RESOURCES

NEWS AND EVENTS

CORPORATE PARTNERS

Beyond slogans . . . Beyond rallies

You can make a real
difference this Earth Day

Join the "A Million Trees for Earth Day" campaign.
It's a gift to the Earth that will last 100 years.

Figure 11. The American Forests Website makes an appeal that is "beyond slogans" but clearly incorporates them, along with the fetish for numbers that includes both trees and time. Reprinted with permission of American Forests.

bilitate federal forestland that has been burned or otherwise damaged. The current leader in the partnership category is the Eddie Bauer Corporation, whose dollar-matching program led to the planting of 4,364,597 trees through February 2001.[39]

The Eddie Bauer effort is part of a larger census of tree planting within the Global ReLeaf campaign, one that has set target goals over the years as high as 100 million trees. By the mid-1990s, that number had been reduced to 20 million trees "by the new millennium," and this goal was used to encourage a rush of tree planting. Membership letters employed the goal of 20 million trees, and the import of the millennium, to motivate the membership:

> *Last year brought us over a million trees closer to realizing our goal* of planting 20 million trees for the new millennium through our *Global ReLeaf 2000* campaign. *We planted 1.4 million trees in 1997*, bringing our total to more than six million trees planted so far. . . . So *take a bow, the credit belongs to you.* Because so many of you responded generously to our pleas to help the environment, we are slowly closing in on our goal.

Unfortunately, "slowly" is the key phrase here. The millennium is right in front of us. That means *we have only three years to plant 14 million trees.* More than 4,500,000 trees per year.[40]

American Forests asked members to contribute to the running total via donations to the organization and by independently planting trees. Initially, "self-planted" trees were to be reported in writing, along with various descriptive details intended to verify that the planting had actually occurred. In 1997, an interactive "Count My Trees!" Website was designated to record and tally this type of planting and add it to the Global ReLeaf total.[41]

That year, I had planted several hundred trees with a retired colleague on his nearby farm, and in order to test the site, I entered them on the Count My Trees! Web page. The planting total listed did, in fact, instantly increase by that amount. To my surprise, the number I entered led to our designation as "among the most prodigious planters to record" a tree-planting effort, and a story appeared in *American Forests,* the first in a series intended to "salute some of those helping make Global ReLeaf 2000's 20-million-trees goal a reality."[42]

Despite appreciating such "heroics," the organization preferred donations and sponsored group activities as the vehicles for pushing Global ReLeaf toward the 20-million millennial goal (the millennium mark has passed, but the program continues). The basic package of ten dollars for ten trees is a minimum, of course, and supporters are encouraged to "plant" twenty trees, thirty trees, or an acre of trees (five hundred) through their donations. The language is calculated to elicit a larger donation while, at the same time, honoring the smaller donations. Eddie Bauer's Global ReLeaf literature states, "Just one tree can make a difference!" alongside the growing number of trees planted through their program.[43] The touted effect, however, is not modest: the text of one advertisement for the company's tree planting promotion reads, "Classic *green,* long-lasting, may *save* the planet. A bargain at *just $1*. It's probably the *best deal* you'll get all day."[44] Pressing the numbers more than the details, Global ReLeaf's solicitations of its members offer transformation of the environment and the planet while sidestepping significant details. For example, one letter asks the question (and then answers it) *"Will we be able to reduce the effects of global climate change? One person can make a difference. A lot of people can make a BIG difference."*[45]

In determining the number of trees that should be planted to offset global climate change, Global ReLeaf offers a deal tailored to the individual. As long as the science of global warming holds that the pace of carbon buildup can be significantly slowed by an increase in the number of trees, a role in stemming the atmospheric carbon increase is available to anyone with a seedling. According to the American Forests Website, "The average American is responsible for about 10 tons of CO_2 emissions. You can plant 30 Global ReLeaf trees right now to offset that annual carbon debt."[46] An alternative to assuming that one is average is to use the organization's Climate Change Calculator to gauge one's individual or corporate debt and remediation figures. An interactive Web page takes detailed information on fuel used in heating and for lawn mowers and leaf blowers, on waste generation (in pounds), on disposal of refrigeration units, on miles driven and miles per gallon for cars, on air travel and other travel, and so on. After entering the information, the user can click to "graphically see your CO_2 and the number of trees that will counteract it." The next "click" option is labeled "I want to plant my trees now."[47]

In recent years, the organization has begun to urge the planting of three trees for each one intended to sequester carbon, in order to insure the full benefit that comes with maturity—with forty years' worth of growth. Thus when one attends to the small print, thirty trees planted secure only ten "trees' worth" of sequestration. Of course, this suggests that one must donate ninety trees to clear the average carbon debt, but thirty is the number more clearly suggested by Global ReLeaf as a suitable payment for a year's consumption. The numbers are fuzzy at best, as no information is offered on tree type, location, care, and the ultimate fate of the mature tree. The numbers involved, and the Climate Change Calculator and its prescription, provide a veneer of science and seriousness, but the fetish of numbers—also common to the timber industry and the government—offers more form than substance. And, once again, they focus attention on remediation, on dealing with the problem after its creation—an avenue facilitated by American Forests while the root causes remain largely unaddressed.

MULTIPLE BENEFITS

"American Forests trees make a world of difference because we plant the right trees in the right places for the right reasons," claims an insert that regularly appears in the *American Forests* journal. The claim is backed by a list labeled "10 Reasons to Plant Trees with American Forests." Though the list is lengthy, its inclusion is warranted inasmuch as it captures many of the stated benefits that pervade the tree planting discourse across groups and sectors. In fact, only reasons six and ten of the list are specific to American Forests. The rest are shared—and claimed—widely:

1. Trees clean our water, and make it safe for drinking, boating, and swimming.

2. Trees clean the air of pollutants and give off oxygen, so we all breathe easier.

3. Trees cool the air, land, and water with shade.

4. Trees provide vital habitat for wildlife, from birds to bears to salamanders, including many endangered and threatened species.

5. Trees save money by reducing the cost of storm water runoff, reducing home and office energy use, and improving property values.

6. Trees count! Every tree you plant counts toward our 20 million goal for the new millennium.

7. Trees celebrate life. Planting trees shares the joy of a birth or birthday, remembers a loved one, or says "thank you" to a friend.

8. Trees make good neighbors. They improve the quality of life, build community spirit, reduce crime, and can help control suburban sprawl.

9. Trees fight climate change by taking carbon from the air. Planting 30 trees each year offsets the average American's "carbon debt"—the amount of carbon dioxide you produce each year from your car and home.

10. It's easy! Just return the card . . . [etc.] Every dollar you contribute plants another tree![48]

Beyond the benefits described in advertisements and promotions, American Forests explores the benefits of trees and its planting programs in frequent articles and updates in *American Forests*. These slightly more detailed and seemingly scientific lists of benefits are offered with brief explanations. The stated benefits include oxygen replenishment, carbon dioxide sequestration, groundwater filtration, pollution control, aesthetics, education, mental health, floodwater control, mineral and nutrients cycling and retention, climate control, habitat for wildlife, physical health and recreation, natural sources of medicines, economy, soil retention, and rejuvenation.[49] However they are couched and presented, the benefits offered by American Forests and by the National Arbor Day Foundation are both comprehensive and far-reaching. Tree planting is depicted as being multidimensional, as operating at various scales, and as holding nearly infinite promise. American Forests notes that "everyone wants to save the world," and that its tree planting programs are a "way to get started."[50]

At times, that starting point is presented as an obligation as much as an opportunity. One advertisement in the organization's journal asks, "Chevrolet/Geo Environmental, American Forests and The National Fish & Wildlife Foundation are helping to make the world a better place to live . . . but is it thanks to you?"[51] Though the advertisement encourages tree planting, its first option states, "If you've purchased a new Chevrolet/Geo car or truck, making it possible for Chevrolet/Geo dealers to support environmental restoration and education . . . The answer is yes."[52] By consuming properly, we do our part in saving the world.

Other proposed obligations disguised as benefits, at least as they are sometimes presented, relate to endangered species and habitats that can be "saved" through tree planting. Many of these are endangered in the sense that they are approaching extinction; at other times, the examples offered are more plebian. An interesting case in point is Walden Woods, an area associated with Thoreau that is threatened by typical urban development. In conjunction with the locally mounted Walden Woods Project and a bevy of celebrities (spearheaded by rocker Don Henley, and including Bette Midler, Jeff Bridges, Jon Lovitz, and many others), American Forests is trying to purchase the land to prevent its loss or conversion.

Under the headline "Help Us Save Walden Woods," readers of American Forests' journal are offered, for thirty-five dollars, a tree "grown from the seed collected from the trees that grow in Walden Woods," so that they can "enjoy Walden's beauty at their own homes." The tag line on the advertisement notes that profits from the sale will help keep "Walden Woods from being paved over and lost forever." It goes on to say, "We need your help, so plant a little heaven in your own backyard."[53] The conjunction of warning, guilt, and association with Walden, Thoreau, and "heaven" constitutes a remarkably manipulative package ripe with symbolism. Expiation of guilt is another of the many benefits of tree planting.

CORPORATE OUTREACH

Another regularly promoted element of Global ReLeaf is its constellation of partners in its programs. An example of this type of promotion was a project to reforest fire-scarred tribal land in New Mexico, which drew upon members of the Mescalero Apache nation, the Bureau of Indian Affairs, and American Forests, and which was sponsored by the Eddie Bauer Corporation.[54] Other projects operated under the Global ReLeaf banner include tree planting with schoolchildren, inner-city youths, indigenous communities in the United States and abroad, and a host of other groups, in conjunction with a range of government agencies and nongovernmental organizations. When such programs are carried out—and publicized—there is often a corporate or governmental underwriter, sometimes several of each.

While the very fact of such partnerships is presented as praiseworthy, American Forests is explicit about the benefits that accrue from them. When the organization approaches potential sponsors for support, it speaks to them of profit more than environmental impacts. The language of these appeals is revealing, and it bears exploration at some length. Under the banner headline "What Corporations Can Do," the organization supplies the answer: "Plant a tree. Grow your market." It goes on to explain:

> American Forests has a long history of working with all segments of society to help people improve the environment with trees and forests. We have worked successfully with a range of companies to promote constructive environmental action that is tangible and nonconfrontational.

Marketing partnerships with American Forests help to build a unique brand awareness, enhance corporate identity, and strengthen consumer and employee loyalty. American Forests can provide substantial opportunities for corporate involvement with a local, national, or global focus.[55]

In answer to the question "Why Work with American Forests?" potential sponsors are told, "Regulation is moving businesses toward environmentally sound practices, but consumer demand and market forces are moving faster. 80% of consumers prefer companies that are associated with a conservation group."[56] The organization provides details to bolster this claim, saying that partnership with the organization can provide the following benefits:

- American Forests' simple, tangible and noncontroversial tree planting message, which has proven effective in consumer and employee promotions
- Use of the American Forests and Global ReLeaf logos on products
- Increased sales
- Public relations and media outreach opportunities
- A unique brand identity, which is tied to improving the environment and reinforces the relationships with consumers and employees[57]

In addition, the organization provides "research findings" that "show that a company's positive environmental actions influence consumer perceptions of products and services and can ultimately affect purchasing decisions." Indeed, "Americans are concerned about the environment and want corporations to help solve environmental problems." It cites a range of studies and statistics showing that, for instance, "two out of every three consumers (69%) purchase certain brands for their connections to worthy causes," that "70% of Americans believe that partnerships between corporations and conservation groups are a highly effective means of protecting the environment," and that "80% of Americans say they have more positive feelings about companies that are in some way associated with environmental groups."[58] The pitch to corporations also emphasizes the enhanced loyalty of employees, who will be more productive and identify more closely with their corporate parent figure on account of the tree planting.

The partnership between the organization and corporations is regularly reported in *American Forests*, under headlines such as "Corporations Go Green," along with information about the partners and the planting programs. For instance, readers are informed, about Mobil, that "the international oil and petrochemical company has as one of its goals to help restore forest ecosystems to health."[59] Eddie Bauer's chief executive officer is quoted as saying, "I am confident that[,] by the year 2000[,] Eddie Bauer, in partnership with American Forests, will have made a real difference in protecting the environment."[60] Of course, what that "real difference" might be is left as an assertion based on the premise that both science and sentiment pronounce tree planting "good," and therefore, that planting trees makes one—whether an individual or a corporation— green. The journal asserts that a "healthy planet" equals "good business," that "tree planting resonates with companies because trees offer a positive environmental impact"—the simple and seemingly obvious part of the equation—and that it is, "therefore[,] a 'no regrets' approach to climate change," at least for those who profit from the association with trees.[61] The role of American Forests, as a broker of contact and cooperation among and between disparate groups, sectors, and perspectives, is to stimulate, organize, ratify, and publicize this "greening" through planting trees, and to package it within millennial symbolism (which, admittedly, may have held more power prior to the event than after) and attach it to the number fetish that amplifies the meaning of one or many trees (see fig. 12).

THE CONTEXT OF GLOBAL RELEAF

If American Forests were nothing more than a shill for corporate interests, the power of the organization and its Global ReLeaf program as a hegemonic vehicle would be greatly reduced. But precisely because the organization functions in its traditional spheres of policy advocacy and technical education, it provides an attractive mechanism for serving its

"*It's great! You just tell him how much pollution your company is responsible for and he tells you how many trees you have to plant to atone for it.*"

Figure 12. One American Forests board member sent this *New Yorker* cartoon to another to express concern about the image and ethics of the Global ReLeaf program. © The New Yorker Collection, 1989, Ed Fisher, from cartoonbank.com. All rights reserved.

traditional forestry constituency. At the same time, through Global ReLeaf, it creates a joint venture that channels the energy of the environmental community, governmental agencies, and corporate power, creating in part, and controlling in part, the symbols deployed in the discourse of trees and nature.

According to its executive director, Deborah Gangloff, American Forests is the "voice of the trees,"[62] and that role confirms its claims about forests and the environment. Indeed, the organization deploys its status as the "oldest conservation organization in America" to add gravitas to its research and advocacy, and legitimacy to its programs. The journal *American Forests* still conveys the organization's work on urban forestry issues, on testimony and expertise offered in Washington on questions relating to the management of public and private lands, and on matters of concern to small woodlot owners.[63] Such material is interspersed with articles and announcements about Global ReLeaf and with advertisements from program sponsors, service providers, and timber and other wood products companies (for example, see fig. 13). Through the forum of *American Forests,* the organization provides the conservation voice (with an occasional advertisement from the National Tree Trust, discussed in the next chapter), and big industry takes out full-page advertisements to celebrate its role as environmental steward. For example, in an ad, the Champion International Corporation, a periodic donor of the paper on which the journal is printed, tells the journal's readers that the corporation has "a big stake in protecting the environment. That's why we know it's important for us to provide proof not only of our good intentions, but also [of] our actual performance."[64]

One message of American Forests, particularly evident in Global ReLeaf but in its other programs and venues as well, is that we can "have it all." Specific threats are identified, and particular solutions are prescribed: plant trees and more trees. While at some level "we" are all cast as part of the problem—because, for example, we generate carbon—the clear emphasis is on our potential role in remediating the symptoms. Occasionally, in the "small print," the organization notes the complexity of the ecosystems, which do not lend themselves to quick fixes, or acknowledges that there is a broader environmental context in which tree

Figure 13. This advertisement in the winter 1996 issue of *American Forests* notes in a caption that the grandmothers of the children pictured here work in an International Paper tree nursery, and that on company tree farms "crops [trees] are harvested and replanted in 25- to 50-year cycles." Reprinted with permission of International Paper.

planting may not be the highest priority. But this type of information is rarely more than a caveat. On the issue of carbon sequestration, a point of some controversy and a major motivation in the Global ReLeaf campaign, Gangloff noted in an interview that, if the science is "wrong" and trees are not useful in combating global warming, "what will we have done? Planted a lot of trees. It's a no-lose situation."[65] The message that the system is complex, and that some of the global benefits may not, in fact, accrue, will likely be missed by the casual participant in the tree planting cause, and is not offered at all to the general public targeted by Global ReLeaf's mass-media outreach.

The overt message of the organization has come to be the primacy of tree planting, the multiple benefits that come with trees, and the efficacy that planting them offers. To reach the widest possible audience, Global ReLeaf is adaptable, ready to fit the needs of donors, locales, and singular events, such as the millennial turn. It should be recalled that the appeal of the program is bound to the broader role of trees in our society and culture. To be the "voice of the trees" is a profound and powerful position, and American Forests works hard to promote trees and their grandeur, within and beyond Global ReLeaf. Two ways of enshrining the tree as an icon are American Forests' Champion Tree and Famous and Historic Tree programs.

Whereas the National Arbor Day Foundation held an election to select *the* National Tree (in terms of species), American Forests keeps an annual list of champions, meticulously tracking the largest specimen of many tree species at both the national and state levels.[66] While this gives some "personality" to specific trees and taps patriotic and chauvinistic impulses, the Famous and Historic Tree program goes a little further: it anthropomorphizes trees in an innovative and commercially successful way. Just as one can purchase a tree that springs from the Walden Woods, so too one can own trees associated with a range of distinguished Americans in categories that include authors, presidents, Native Americans, women, African Americans, and figures associated with particular events or periods, like the Civil War. The more macabre can purchase a Texas "hanging oak." On a more uplifting note, trees associated with Gifford Pinchot and John Audubon are available, as are trees to commemorate John Chapman (Johnny Appleseed to most). There are also the Elvis Presley pin oaks, sweetgums, weeping willows, and sycamores, all taken from the grounds of Graceland and ready to provide a "living link to the greatest entertainer of all time" (see fig. 14).[67] For those who feel that Elvis is too frivolous a symbol, there are the "trees to remember a world at war," the Eisenhower green ash trees—part of a nationwide Operation Silent Witness memorial campaign. That program was inaugurated in the Arlington National Cemetery and will spread to 10,000 Veterans of Foreign Wars posts throughout the country to connect trees with patriotism and commemoration—through the support of Wal-Mart and the Scotts Company, and in conjunction with the White House and the U.S. Department of Agriculture's Millennium Green Project.[68] The terrorist attacks of September 11, 2001, can also be memorialized through tree planting, as pointed out by Deborah Gangloff in the 2002 annual report of the National Urban and Community Forestry Advisory Council.[69]

LOCAL RELIEF

For the time being, Global ReLeaf has provided American Forests with a measure of success and influence, allowing the organization to shift from a survival to a growth mode. Though it did not achieve its magic number of 20 million trees planted by the millennium, Global ReLeaf has secured a place in the pantheon of nonprofit tree planting programs, and this was surely a primary goal for American Forests. With its newfound support, the organization may seek to be the voice of the trees, yet it seems to speak in the language of the discourse of trees, offering much in return for planting. Despite early concerns that Global ReLeaf was a sham and that it could not deliver on its promises, American Forests creates a space for individuals and groups from across the environmental spectrum to meet and "save the planet."

While the benefits of planting trees are depicted as universal, the most tangible returns from the planting program are for the corporate sponsors of Global ReLeaf. Not only do they increase their profits through a

Figure 14. The Famous and Historic Trees program allows anyone to own a living piece of the Elvis mythology. Reprinted with permission of American Forests.

green affiliation, but they also enhance employee productivity and corporate loyalty. The public is encouraged to reward corporate sponsors through brand-specific consumption and, at a subtle yet compelling level, through the recognition that all those associated with Global ReLeaf are partners in a common effort to restore and improve the environment. Members too are given the opportunity to pay down their share of the "guilt" in global warming and to purchase a role in saving the planet, all for just ten dollars. The success of American Forests and its tree planting program comes at least in part through the pacification of consumers and workers. Together with corporate interests and the government, the other partners in Global ReLeaf—that is, the general public—may indeed be planting the future.

FIVE Uncle Sam Plants for You

Trees are always working to help people . . .
they serve you every day.

U.S. Forest Service

Like other functions of government in the United States, tree planting is spread among many agencies, and it involves overlapping sets of employees and politicians, different bodies of legislation, budgets that rise and fall, evolving agendas, and sometimes, competing interest groups. The primary governmental agency for developing and implementing policy for trees and forests is the U.S. Forest Service, but the question of who does what, and why, is complicated. This chapter examines elements of the government that support tree planting both directly and indirectly, and it focuses on areas of interface with nonprofit tree planters in both practical and conceptual terms.

Because the range and history of the government's involvement in tree planting, and in environmental issues generally, are sprawling and complex, my survey is in some respects only cursory. My goal is not, however, to be comprehensive, as that would involve a work of encyclopedic length, but rather to convey a sense of the many sources and methods of government support, as well as describe how this support is generated, organized, delivered, and communicated. A common current running through governmental participation in tree planting is the language used to explain, justify, and promote the many programs in the country and the role of trees in managing the environment.

Like the National Arbor Day Foundation and American Forests, government agencies—whether local, state, or federal—tap into the discourse of trees, speaking in terms of partnership, multiple benefits, and the sense of efficacy created in participants, and employing the fetish of numbers. When this message comes from a governmental source, it carries the weight of authority and is backed by the resources of the state. One striking example comes from the Environmental Protection Agency, nominally the flagship governmental body entrusted with creating stewardship policy and authorized to monitor its implementation. On its Website, the agency offers the list "Things You Can Do to Help Stop Global Warming" under the heading "The Power of Planting Trees." The list is similar to that tendered by American Forests, matching various carbon-producing activities with the number of trees needed to offset the carbon generated by them.

There is a certain tone of luxury in the Environmental Protection Agency's list of carbon-generating activities, which includes motorcycle riding, jet skiing, pleasure boating, cruise ship trips, and air travel, tacitly directing attention to vacation and recreation activities rather than daily life. The language of some of the additional categories is interesting and extends this theme:

Paper: Plant three trees to offset the 613 pounds of paper one person uses in a typical year[.] (Remember those maps, brochures and flyers that you collected while on vacation? *Plant some trees and stop feeling guilty about all the trees that die to distribute that information!*)

Electricity: After every 10,000 kilowatt-hours, plant 10 trees[.] (One tree every 1,000 kilowatt-hours. *We use electricity everywhere, so use it without guilt by planting trees!*)[1]

The agency even offers a pay-in-advance plan, suggesting, "For a car getting 15 miles per gallon, you should plant 320 trees (a one-time purchase of 200 trees will absorb 5 tons of carbon dioxide each year for the next 40 years . . .)."[2] Under the banner headline "Individuals Can Make a Difference," it encourages this palliative tree planting and provides a Web link to the American Forests Website.[3] Though planting groups rarely speak out quite as explicitly as the agency does when it advises people to "stop feeling guilty," that same message is implicit in much of the tree planting discourse.

The idea that trees can make things better, and therefore that one can continue to consume without guilt, is powerful. It takes on additional legitimacy because it is conveyed in the context of supporting the nonprofit tree planting sector and represented as stewardship of natural resources. I trace the functions and language of planters from the federal on down to the municipal level, particularly as they network with nongovernmental planters at the local level, in order to demonstrate the role of government in contributing to a platform of environmental management through tree planting. I then turn to the local nongovernmental groups that carry out these programs and disseminate their message, and that are the recipients of government and corporate guidance and, at times, financial support.

Across this range of participants, the consistency of the message—both its content and its ubiquitous deployment—reveals the ongoing construction and use of a hegemonic discourse of trees and nature. As noted by Gramsci, the mechanism of hegemony links the state and capital with the general population through civil society, in this case institutions and associations like the tree planting groups. Some of the support for the groups comes from the grassroots, but much of the language, and the money, comes from government sources. Rather than tracking down every government agency involved, such as the Natural Resources Conservation Service, the Bureau of Land Management, and other departments and agencies that have a small role in tree planting, I focus on the Forest Service as both a key source of the planting discourse and an exemplar of the forms that it takes and its functions.

THE FOREST SERVICE: FROM TOP TO BOTTOM

Though the Forest Service remains the branch of the federal government responsible for the bulk of reforesting of public lands, the number of trees planted has dipped as timber harvesting in national forests has decreased. In 1998, Forest Service nurseries produced nearly 62 million seedlings. While this is a prodigious number, only 4 percent of the total number of seedling produced that year came from nurseries operated by the Forest Service and other federal agencies. Moreover, projects on federal public land covered roughly one-tenth the acreage planted in the private sector.[4] The Forest Service is applying its technical and financial support in other areas of forestry, extending its reach and influence into the commercial, non-profit, and public sectors, far beyond the boundaries of the national forests.

The part of the Forest Service most directly relevant to the broad community of tree planters is the State and Private Forestry Division. The mandate of the Forest Service as a whole, as articulated by its first head, Gifford Pinchot, was to "provide the greatest amount of good to the greatest amount of people for the long run." State and Private Forestry "cooperates with State and local governments, forest industries, other private landowners and forest users in the management, protection, and development of forest land in non-Federal ownership."[5] It also coordinates and funds the assistance delivered both directly and through state foresters to groups like the National Arbor Day Foundation and American Forests, and is in charge of planting programs specifically aimed at fulfilling governmental commitments, whether formal or informal, to reduce the emission of greenhouse gasses in accordance with international agreements. Within the State and Private Forestry Division, the most pertinent branch is Cooperative Forestry, which maintains a wide range of programs that assist with tree planting activities.[6]

COOPERATIVE FORESTRY

Across the range of Cooperative Forestry programs (expanded under the 1978 Cooperative Forestry Assistance Act), the government provides three main types of support: financial, technical, and informational or educational.[7] Many of the programs are designed to be accessible to the general public, while others coordinate or support the activities of other federal, state, and local government agencies or nongovernmental organizations. There are two primary constituencies for Cooperative Forestry programs. First are the owners of nonindustrial private forests—that is, those landowners who sell their trees to others for manufacturing wood and paper products, as opposed to timber and paper companies, which sell products manufactured from their own trees as well as purchase timber from others. Second, and more relevant to this study, are the residents of towns and cities across the country who benefit from urban forests. The needs of these two groups differ widely.

According to the Forest Service, the management of private forestland in the United States "impact[s] the social, economic, and natural environment for everyone."[8] To have an active role on private lands, beyond the legislative role that affects land management, the Forest Service creates and administers programs that channel assistance to rural communities and private landowners to foster the growth and maintenance of timber stock. The programs are couched in terms of stewardship and management and are designed to keep the land in timber production for the long-term, though that term is not particularly well defined. Effectively, the intent is to make forestry profitable and "sustainable," another term that has, at best, circular definitions within the Forest Service and its programs, as its meaning has ever been formalized. The Cooperative Forestry program's slogan is: "Connecting People to Resources, Ideas, and One Another So They Can Care for Forests and Sustain Their Communities." Among the overarching goals of the program is to "help produce a variety of forest-based goods and services to meet domestic and international needs."[9]

To do this, Cooperative Forestry runs various programs, including the Economic Action Programs, the Landowner Assistance Programs, the Rural Forestry Assistance Programs, the National Resources Conservation and Education Program, the Forestry Legacy Program, and the Urban and Community Forestry Program. Among these, Rural Forestry Assistance Programs have one of the larger and broader constellations, offering a range of direct and indirect support through the "application of sound environmental and economic resource management principles."[10]

RURAL FORESTRY ASSISTANCE PROGRAMS

The Forest Resource Management program provides technical assistance on various aspects of timber growth, including tree planting and harvesting and the subsequent planting of more trees. The Forestry Incentives Program offers financial, technical, and educational support to encourage landowners to grow trees on open or formerly forested and underforested lands. Under this program, the Forest Service, working through the state foresters, provides grants to nonindustrial, private forest landowners who have as much as a thousand acres of land that could be reforested. The program supplies up to 75 percent of the cost of planting trees, with a ten-thousand-dollar maximum, conditional on the land remaining in the program for at least ten years. In discussing the Forestry Incentives Program, the Forest Service notes that, "besides timber production, healthy productive forests also provide many other public goods: such as, watershed protection, wildlife habitat, aesthetics, and recreational activities."[11]

The Forest Service also recognizes profit as an important motive for keeping the forests in production, thus another element of support offered by Cooperative Forestry's Rural Forestry Assistance Programs is the Forest Taxation Program, which provides information and tips on minimizing cost and maximizing yield in relation to the tax code. The first point offered to landowners, for instance, is that they "can claim a 10% reforestation tax credit and a 7-year amortization for qualified reforestation expenses." However, the program information also notes, "You must have a profit motive to claim business or investment expenses," a reminder that the business of trees is, first and foremost, timber production.[12]

Trees used to support these programs are grown by state agencies with the support of the Reforestation, Nursery, and Genetic Resources program, which provides technical support and material for local cultivation. Seed for the latter program comes from the National Tree Seed

Laboratory, a part of the U.S. Forest Service. The lab specializes in generating, preserving, and selling high quality tree seed to private landowners and nurseries throughout the country. According to the lab's mission statement:

> Worldwide and national interest in planting trees is at an all-time high. Campaigns carried out by such groups as American Forests (Global ReLeaf) and the National Arbor Day Foundation are signs of this high interest. The success of these and other planting programs depends on high-quality seedlings—good seedlings start with high quality seed. The mission of the National Tree Seed Laboratory is to assist in providing a quality start for global reforestation.[13]

Much is contained in this statement, which asserts a tacit link between individual members of tree planting organizations and both national and worldwide efforts for "global reforestation"; indeed, it is such membership that has pushed the interest to "an all-time high." Further evidence that the Forest Service endorses and tangibly supports tree planting organizations is the fact that the National Tree Seed Laboratory's Website, in addition to highlighting American Forests and the National Arbor Day Foundation and providing links to their Websites, bears their organizational emblems. In this way, the imprint of the source—the federal government—helps to make the nonprofit groups "official" partners in the cause. This gives credence to the institutions of civil society, identified by Gramsci as the agencies that reach out to and enlist the general public in discourses that mold public opinion and create consensus.

URBAN AND COMMUNITY FORESTRY PROGRAM

Out of the Forest Service's total budget of $3.5 billion in 2000, the cost of Cooperative Forestry programs, excluding the Urban and Community Forestry Program, totaled roughly only $83 million.[14] The latter program is a result of a congressional act stipulating in part that

1. the health of forests in urban areas and communities, including cities, their suburbs, and towns, in the United States is on the decline;

2. forest lands, shade trees, and open spaces in urban areas and communities improve the quality of life for residents;

3. forest lands and associated natural resources enhance the economic value of residential and commercial property in urban and community settings;

4. urban trees are 15 times more effective than forest trees at reducing the buildup of carbon dioxide and aid in promoting energy conservation through mitigation of the heat island effect in urban areas;

5. tree plantings and ground covers such as low growing dense perennial turfgrass sod in urban areas and communities can aid in reducing carbon dioxide emissions, mitigating the heat island effect, and reducing energy consumption, thus contributing to efforts to reduce global warming trends;

6. efforts to encourage tree plantings and protect existing open spaces in urban areas and communities can contribute to the social well-being and promote a sense of community in these areas; and

7. strengthened research, education, technical assistance, and public information and participation in tree planting and maintenance programs for trees and complementary ground covers for urban and community forests are needed to provide for the protection and expansion of tree cover and open space in urban areas and communities.[15]

Though Congress is not typically thought of as a tree planting agency, it does authorize the funding for governmental work of this type and, through legislation, has translated the benefits of tree planting into law.

In general terms, "urban forestry is the comprehensive management of forests and related natural resources in populated areas, from the inner city, to the developing fringe, to small outlying communities."[16] The Urban and Community Forestry Program is charged with helping "State forestry agencies, local and tribal governments, and the private sector improve natural resource management of trees and forests in urban areas and community settings."[17] According to a Forest Service publication, the work is important because "the vitality of our communities is strongly dependent on the quality of the natural environment—the green infrastructure."[18] To discharge its mandate, the program delivers money, information, and technical advice through a variety of channels, all geared to stimulate and organize the effort to plant and maintain trees in over ten thousand communities across the United States and its territories.

In order to promote the program's work, the Forest Service invokes the value of trees to the community and individuals. According to program materials, "The basis for the value of an urban tree could be emotional, aesthetic, or it could be strictly utilitarian. However, people seldom perceive value as strictly aesthetic or monetary. There is often substantial overlap that makes 'value' difficult to classify."[19] This does not stop the Urban and Community Forestry Program from discussing the economic advantages of trees in all the myriad forms they may take. The program provides extensive information on how to determine the approximate worth of a tree in dollar terms, citing as a source a publication titled *Valuation of Landscape Trees, Shrubs, and Other Plants: A Guide to the Methods and Procedures for Appraising Amenity Plants.*[20] The program's Website provides an example that calculates the value of a particular hypothetical tree by drawing on size, condition, species, and location, producing—in their sample case—a value of $2,437 for an individual tree. In a statement that recalls the "trees raise property values" approach taken by American Forests and the National Arbor Day Foundation, a technical guide produced by the Urban and Community Forestry Program points out that "local governments capture some of this monetary value because property values increase assessed values for the tax base."[21] Thus, within the broader list of benefits, specific interests can be targeted, and the financial windfall can be offered as an incentive to urban forestry and municipal officials, who have the most proximate interface with the general public.

Urban and Community Forestry points out other values of urban trees too, and though there is significant overlap with the benefits list propagated by other groups, this governmental view of trees warrants some examination. In an interesting variation from the other lists, program material ranks benefits according to their "measurability." Moving from the least quantifiable to the most, the list includes psychological and aesthetic values, social values, historic values, environmental values, and finally, monetary values. Monetary values are evident in the description and analysis of many of the other types of values as well. For example, "although difficult to gauge, uplifted spirits is one important benefit of trees. Some of the difficulty in measuring these benefits may grow out of society's decision to exclude tree values from the marketplace. Other emotion-based commodities, such as flowers, perfume, view property, prestige automobiles, and entertainment, are readily assigned monetary values. But with proper treatment, researchers can tie monetary values to the emotional benefits of trees."[22]

The desire to quantify the benefits of trees, to treat the benefits as a commodity, reflects an underlying utilitarianism that pervades much of the planting discourse and is a primary motivation for manipulating the environment. Some of the benefits of trees that Urban and Community Forestry reports, however, may be too complex to capture solely through economic consideration, according to the technical guide produced by the program, and when there are local disputes over particularly significant trees, "the issue will usually be settled by public pressure not by market forces."[23] Factors contributing to the power of such trees in the community are their role in creating "community identity," "cooperation," and "symbolic links with the past." Beyond such sentiments, "people value both the aesthetic and physical quality of our environment. Trees contribute to this quality by modifying local climates, reducing noise and air pollution, and by protecting soil and water." A great deal of information is offered on the role of trees in moderating heat in urban areas, reducing noise pollution, and absorbing carbon. On this last point the program offers a mixture of fact, numbers, research, and assertion typical of the tree planting discourse:

> Increasingly, carbon dioxide is being recognized as a "greenhouse gas" pollutant with potentially devastating consequences, such as global warming. . . . Since photosynthesis in green plants consumes carbon dioxide, plants could help to counteract the increase of this gas in the atmosphere. Rosenfeld, Martin, and Rainer report that planting urban trees could reduce heating and cooling demands enough to significantly cut fossil fuel consumption. They suggest that urban trees could be about 10 times as effective as forest trees for lowering carbon dioxide in cities.[24]

Though the benefits of urban forests may seem obvious and far ranging to some, Urban and Community Forestry is engaged in an educational campaign to promote planting programs at the municipal level. The issue is not one of creating a favorable orientation toward trees, as one survey of 566 municipal officials found that 92 percent of them agreed that trees "enhance the quality of life in a community."[25] The challenge is to stimulate implementation of the program's vision in sympathetic communities through the "transfer of knowledge and technology."[26] That transfer contributes to an orthodoxy of sorts, as programs around the country become variants of a standard model of how and why to plant trees. In order to further this effort, the Forest Service looks for and supports additional partners in the educational effort.

THE NATIONAL URBAN AND COMMUNITY FORESTRY ADVISORY COUNCIL

Another avenue for directing education about the planting of trees is the National Urban and Community Forestry Advisory Council, which provides challenge grants to organizations involved in aspects of urban forestry. Two of the council's specific goals are to "stimulate increased funding from traditional and non-traditional sources for planning and planting of high quality new trees" and to "promote private enterprise and homeowners as valuable partners in the preservation and management of urban trees and forests."[27] Deborah Gangloff, executive director of American Forests, began a three-year term as chair of the National Urban and Community Forestry Advisory Council in 1999. In her first annual report as chair, she noted, "There are many partners in the urban forestry movement—individuals, businesses, non-profit organizations, and governments at all levels."[28]

The council sponsors organizations it deems to be engaged in programs that influence urban forestry nationally, and this may include organizations that "either communicate effectively to a large number of people or . . . provide innovative and workable ways to reach specific groups with important and sometimes complex information." Also eligible for funding are projects that "stimulate the development of additional funding for urban forestry through private sector support and local investments, and cultivate private sector partnerships that leverage investments of human and financial resources."[29]

Many groups qualify for and receive support from the National Urban and Community Forestry Advisory Council, among them American Forests and the National Arbor Day Foundation. The secretary of agriculture appoints the council's board of directors according to a formula that mandates distribution of its seats among government, nongovernmental organizations, academia, and businesses. Interlocking relationships and interests, and a common sense of purpose, characterize the community of tree planters that dominates the institutions represented on the board and sets the tone across the planting sectors. The National Arbor Day Foundation, for example, had unofficial representation on the National Urban and Community Forestry Advisory Council Board through one of its academic appointments, James Fazio of the University of Idaho, the primary technical consultant to the foundation and author of many of its newsletter items.

The council is a vehicle for communication and cooperation, and is one way to fund and support the circle of participants in a common endeavor, just as many other interest groups combine government policy makers and researchers, lobbyists, nongovernmental organizations, corporate leaders, and academics. Contact and cooperation can be both formal and informal, but contact is clearly a goal of the council and, more broadly, Cooperative Forestry. The premier gathering of this community is the annual National Urban Forest Conference, hosted and organized by American Forests (its executive director serves as chair of the council) and funded by the Forest Service, the Eddie Bauer Corporation, and the Davey Tree Company. The 2001 conference was held in Washington, D.C., and among the program committee members were staff members of American Forests, the upper echelon of Cooperative Forestry, representatives from regional offices of the Forest Service, state foresters from Texas and Indiana, municipal environmental and forestry staff members, and others. In public meetings such as this conference, the message of tree planting is disseminated with pomp and circumstance and circulated at the national level. The network that convenes at annual urban forestry conferences extends from Washington, D.C., to incorporate a series of facilitators distributed around the country; the next key sector in the chain of participants is the state forester.

THE STATE FORESTER AS CONDUIT

The National Association of State Foresters serves as an important national mechanism for communication about and transmission of forest programs and information, and for allocation of federal funds. The association's programs and committees parallel the divisions and goals of the Forest Service, as does its communications about trees and forests. The association's Urban and Community Forestry program (which operates with support from the U.S. Forest Service's program of the same name) states that "tree planting programs have proven to be one of the most effective vehicles to get community leaders and citizens energized about their natural resources. Trees and their resulting benefits are something to which all people can easily relate. Across the country, tree planting events have repeatedly resulted in the development of grassroots citizen led groups that are committed to the long-term improvement and care of their community's natural resources."[30]

Of course these citizen-led groups are operating with a template, and often funding, provided by the government, thus the leadership still comes at least in part from above. Within each state and U.S. territory, there is a forestry agency with its own programs and policies. In many states, forestry is a separate unit within the government, while in some parts of the country forestry is housed within a department of natural resources or an environmental agency. State forestry programs often are administered by extension service agents or county foresters, particularly in timber producing regions. Like the National Association of State Foresters, state forestry departments often replicate the Forest Service in their programs; thus state forestlands may be their primary responsibility, but they also engage in education, cooperative forestry, and urban forestry. They have a part in the discourse of trees, both in transmitting the message and money of the federal government and in facilitating joint ventures at the local level while generating publicity that encourages and publicizes planting projects.

An example of how agencies and organizations coordinate their efforts is the Washington Community Forestry Council's publication *Community*

Forestry and Urban Growth: A Toolbox for Incorporating Urban Forestry Elements into Community Plans.[31] The report was funded by the Forest Service and the council's parent agency, the Washington Department of Natural Resources. The document provides "residents and planners with suggested wording that will help them incorporate urban forestry elements into their comprehensive plans," and a glossary of terms, "so that we might all begin to speak the same language when discussing trees and their relationship to urban life."[32] These statements pinpoint the part played by such agencies and the programs they sponsor in reinforcing the importance of trees in society and in defining the role that trees have in managing the environment—key elements of the hegemonic discourse.

The list of tree benefits in the report is familiar and includes, among others, the following items:

- Trees increase property values
- Trees increase economic development
- Trees reduce surface water runoff rates and volume
- Trees increase energy-conservation benefits
- Trees are oxygen producers and clean the air
- Trees reduce noise pollution
- Trees are good for our health
- Trees provide wildlife habitat
- Trees maintain and improve surface water quality
- Trees provide a buffer between different land uses
- Trees aid in traffic control
- Trees provide aesthetic screening[33]

Elsewhere in its pages, the document offers similar information under the heading "Facts and Benefits." One fact and benefit is that trees can "help by . . . consuming atmospheric carbon dioxide—a 'greenhouse gas'—an acre of trees inhales the amount of carbon dioxide emitted by a single automobile in one year."[34] Another fact and benefit is that trees contribute by "helping create an enjoyable environment—a Weyer-

haeuser publication refers to a 1986 survey conducted in all 50 states by
the Gallup Organization on the value of landscaping. Overall, buyers of
new and previously owned homes estimated that landscaping added
nearly 15 percent to the value or selling price of their homes."[35] Thus, the
government is reporting from a timber industry publication that relies on
a public opinion survey, all marked by an absence of detail and context.
Yet because the material bears the government's imprint, it gains in credibility and promotes the relationship and image of the groups mentioned.
It is interesting to note that the appended section "Resources and
References" incorporates material from James Fazio's work for the
National Arbor Day Foundation, a report produced for the U.S. Department of Energy by an American Forests vice president, many papers
from National Urban Forest Conference proceedings and other American
Forests materials, and a number of Forest Service documents and studies
as well.

The neighboring state of Oregon has produced a similar report published by an adjunct of the Oregon Department of Forestry. The Oregon
Urban and Community Forest Council, now called Oregon Community
Trees, is a nonprofit organization established by the Oregon Department
of Forestry to advise it on urban forest issues. Membership in Oregon
Community Trees is open to the public but requires an annual membership fee of thirty dollars. Publications and reports issued by the program
carry the imprint of the Oregon Department of Forestry, and both bodies
acknowledge that the budget for work done by Oregon's Urban and
Community Forestry Assistance Program comes from the Forest Service's
Cooperative Forestry program.

Oregon Community Trees urges the state's communities to participate
in the National Arbor Day Foundation's Tree City USA program, and one
of its publications cites benefits of urban planting that have been
reported in material authored by the staff of American Forests.[36] It also
recommends participation in American Forests' programs and those of
the National Tree Trust, discussed below. The message of Oregon
Community Trees and its publications is a familiar one, illustrated by
Seeing the Forests for the Trees, which quotes Rick Zenn, education director
for the World Forestry Center in Portland, Oregon: "I strongly believe

that planting and maintaining trees in our own communities is one of the most effective ways to connect people, like you and me, to the larger global environment we all inhabit."[37]

Along with offering a list of benefits that trees provide, Oregon Community Trees calls for partnerships with organizations like American Forests and companies like the Louisiana-Pacific Corporation, and it raises funds to support the urban forest. Lamenting the lack of a big budget to support its program, which the government could provide, it suggests that "unless a dedicated planting fund is established, other private programs such as Global ReLeaf may fill some of this void."[38] In other words, where the government leaves off, the nonprofit tree planting groups will have to step in. Oregon Community Trees has managed to fill that void to some degree with the support of the Louisiana-Pacific timber company, which funded the publication of its community forestry report, adding another dimension to the partnerships it fosters.

The regular newsletter of the program, which Oregon Community Trees produces jointly with the Urban and Community Forestry Division of the Oregon Department of Forestry, supplies information on how to qualify for Tree City USA status, applications for funding by the National Tree Trust, a version of the Climate Change Calculator devised by American Forests that calculates "trees per miles driven," copies of winning entries in the National Arbor Day Foundation poster contest, and information on how to contact these organizations. In Oregon, as in all the states, a member of the Department of Forestry—often one employed in an urban forestry section—serves as state coordinator for the National Arbor Day Foundation's Tree City USA program.

State forestry programs across the country have a basic set of administration functions: they manage state forests, support the owners of nonindustrial private forestry lands, and provide advice and funding to municipalities and nonprofit groups for urban and community forests. The Forest Service is a partner in many of these activities and is always present in the urban and community forestry programs, at least as a contributor of funds, though often in an advisory capacity too. The National Arbor Day Foundation and American Forests also make regular appearances in the materials issued by state forestry programs, as partners with and resources for the general public. On its Website, the Kansas Forest Service, for instance, prominently displays the symbol of the National Arbor Day Foundation and offers a biography of J. Sterling Morton, a template that communities and states can use to create an Arbor Day proclamation, and links to the foundation's Website.

Many state forestry agencies also manage tree nurseries. Often they channel surplus trees, via the state forester, to nonprofit groups and municipalities at a discount, or even for free, in order to help them carry out programs inspired by or mounted in conjunction with American Forests or National Arbor Day Foundation projects. Whether they provide trees, transmit federal aid, or furnish technical and educational advice to tree planting groups, the state foresters act as a conduit from the national to the local level, where the planting programs are implemented. By the time the message and material get to the local level, tree planting is a largely homogenized endeavor accompanied by both bureaucracy and money. The standardized discourse of trees is part of a message stating that individuals can be partners in, and can benefit from, the expert stewardship of nature that comes with government specialists and government planting programs.

GREENING THE NEIGHBORHOODS: TOWN AND CITY PLANTING

By 2001, more than twenty-five hundred communities, with a combined population of over 80 million residents, had qualified for Tree City USA standing with the National Arbor Day Foundation. As noted in chapter 3, qualifying towns and cities have met requirements related to tree planting that include passing a tree ordinance, maintaining a budget for trees and tree care, promoting Arbor Day, and having a legal body to preside over these matters. The fact of earning Tree City USA status indicates a relationship between a municipal government, the National Association of State Foresters, and the National Arbor Day Foundation. Money flows to the state from the Forest Service and is passed on at the local level to the municipal government and, at times, nonprofit tree planting organizations.

Local tree planters have an advantage in being able to provide a critical product—the tree. In some cities, when trees are threatened by storms, pests, or the encroachment of urban sprawl, they become part of the urban agenda. In these cases, the urban forester is likely to find widespread support in replacing sick or damaged trees. Despite their appeal for many communities, however, trees are neglected in comparison with other elements of the urban infrastructure that demand money and attention. In either case, the urban forester must, like any other bureaucrat, make an argument for a budget and undertake outreach to maintain public support. As a result, urban foresters often adopt the discourse of other planting bodies and sell their communities on the benefits of trees. In commercial areas, they tout the economic benefits and, in large cities, the effect on heat and cooling. At the local level, they emphasize some of the less tangible consequences. For example, the Georgia Forestry Commission observes that "active involvement in tree planting programs has been shown to enhance a community's sense of social identity, self-esteem, and territoriality, and *it teaches residents that they can work together to choose and control the conditions of their environment*.[39]

One indicator of how communities can "choose and control" their environment, or at least manipulate its image, is the language of their planting programs. The nomenclature of municipal programs, and of the local programs that partner with them, reveals this desire. "Neighborwoods," for example, a term for the urban place where people live that also signals their desire to live in a more forested location, is the name of a municipal planting program in my own town of Eugene, Oregon, and in others, including Olympia, Chicago, Austin, Raleigh, Fayetteville, Sacramento, and many smaller communities. Across the country, there are nonprofit groups with similar names, among them Green Leaf, TreePeople, Tree Musketeers, Treemendus, Trees Are Us, Trees Please, Trees Forever, Trees For the Future, American Treedition, Up With Trees!, and Tree Action. Often it is these nongovernmental partners in local planting efforts that carry the discourse of trees to the community, where they find citizens who will embrace it.

CITIZEN PLANTERS

There are two key components to understanding local groups and their role in the transmission of the tree planting discourse. The first is the literature of self-help and advice that has been produced by and for other tree planters, and the second is the material produced by the local groups to advertise their own activities and recruit the public. The seminal text for creating a tree planting program or group is a book by Andy and Kate Lipkis, *The Simple Act of Planting a Tree: Healing Your Neighborhood, Your City, and Your World*. In the book's foreword, the environmental oracle Lester Brown, president of the Worldwatch Institute, writes, "In the battle to save the planet, tree planters are on the front lines," and "every tree planted is another step forward" in this battle.[40] This is the flip side of the numbers fetish, of course, investing a single tree, and a single planter, with power. The content of the book itself deals with the formation and functioning of a local tree planting group and is based on the TreePeople organization founded in 1974 by Andy Lipkis.

Lipkis is a legend in tree planting groups, having undertaken the greening of Los Angeles as a fifteen-year-old high school student, ultimately building a coalition of volunteers and supporters that has, at times, captured the attention of a city that lives on image. TreePeople mobilized a million-tree campaign to beautify Los Angeles in preparation for the 1984 Olympic games, and the organization has been in the pantheon of planting groups ever since. According to the authors, tree planting is both profoundly local and personal, and, despite the adulation that has come their way, sparked by such things as an appearance on the *Tonight Show* with Johnny Carson and the support of many Hollywood celebrities, they contend that "everyone who embarks on this [tree-planting] journey is a hero."[41] When the Lipkises share their thoughts about tree planting, they soar to new planes of rhetoric while drawing upon themes of American nationalism and might, which they couch in a language of inclusion and transcendence:

> Planting has the ability to transform our own behavior and that of our culture. *Tree planting takes the simple act of an individual and elevates it,*

revealing the truth about where true power rests in the world. The result of a single person's planting can be monumental, and when the individual acts are added up, the result is powerful evidence of what one can do for the world. For some reason, this work causes people to move beyond political, philosophical, cultural, racial, and economic differences to cooperate together.[42]

Tree planting, they state, provides "internal peace, beauty, safety, joy, simplicity, caring, and satisfaction," and the community of tree planters—the community established through tree planting—can "nurture responsibility for our global environment."[43] With such a recipe, it is no wonder that the work of TreePeople, and the manifesto produced by the heads of the organization, serves as a source of inspiration for those interested in the transformative power of trees or in simply greening up their city. As for the source of true power, it resides more in the discourse and those who deploy it than in the individuals planting trees to beautify their homes.

There are other books of this type, with various approaches to finding potential tree planters. Some of these books are more technical and forestry driven—including one published jointly by American Forests and the National Association of Home Builders.[44] Others are oriented more toward community activism, and one, *Grow Your Own Trees,* comes with over one hundred tree seeds to give the purchaser a start on creating the urban forest.[45] Local planters can also find inspiration in Jean Giono's *The Man Who Planted Trees,* Dr. Seuss's *The Lorax,* Shel Silverstein's *The Giving Tree* (which is not really about tree planting but still gets mentioned as a source of inspiration), and of course, anything about Johnny Appleseed, among many other sources.[46]

Local planting groups do their share of promotion, since generating publicity for tree planting is critical to their success. The language they employ ranges from exact replication of the materials offered by government and national planting organizations to a more tailored and personal message that carries the tone of a community. Sometimes they blend the two, as indicated in the benefits list put together by the Eugene Tree Foundation, which reads in part:

Trees absorb and mute noise from traffic, lawn mowers, skateboards, leaf blowers, boom boxes and other city sounds.

Trees soften the often harsh lines of glass, masonry and steel buildings, cement and asphalt, and all the various other man-made surfaces that function as the urban infrastructure and which have contributed to a certain alienation and apartness from the natural world.

Trees help establish a sense of community within a neighborhood. The Big Leaf Maple outside my house along the park strip is not my tree, or my neighbor's tree. It belongs to everyone who walks or rides by, or as is more likely the case, as the poet Wendell Berry would have it, we belong to it.[47]

Unlike the Eugene Tree Foundation, which conveys detailed concerns, an antiurban bias, and an ecocentric tone, the Trees Atlanta organization speaks in a language of benefits that lists the economic and environmental gains in quantitative terms: dollars saved, carbon sequestered, oxygen manufactured, and so on. Friends of Trees in Portland, Oregon, combines the numbers fetish of tree planting—in their Seed the Future program's goal of 144,000 trees to be planted—with brightly colored artwork depicting the city as an attractive but concrete world being improved by children planting trees (see fig. 15).

Local nonprofit planting groups (there are too many in the United States to mention here) are variations on basic themes—they are not exactly mirror images of one another but draw from similar sources to achieve common ends. There is also a cadre of national-level tree planting organizations that seek support for their cause for particular reasons. Some of these lack the geographic specificity of the local groups; others draw upon a national constituency to support a project in a particular, often special, place.

One of the more esoteric and ambitious of these groups is the Tree of Peace Society, created by Jake Swamp, a chief of the Mohawk Nation in the Iroquois Confederacy, living in New York. The Tree of Peace is an Iroquois tradition in which parties meet beneath a "tree of peace" to resolve the conflicts between them. To foster a spirit of reconciliation, Chief Swamp has taken as his goal the planting of 2 billion trees through-

Figure 15. Max Grover's representation of children planting trees in Portland, Oregon, is part of material promoting the Friends of Trees organization. Reprinted with permission of Friends of Trees.

out the world, in conjunction with local partners, of course. Swamp's work in the United States and many other countries has earned him a media award from the National Arbor Day Foundation, recognition from the White House, and publicity for tree planting in the places chosen for his work.

As an organization, the Colorado-based Plant-It 2000 has a less personal face than local nonprofit planting groups have, but it tries to allow its contributors to have a sense of control by letting donors pick where their donated trees will be planted. For each dollar donated (there is a ten-dollar minimum donation), the group will plant a tree in a location selected from a list of sites in the United States and abroad, with choices possible in Asia, South America, and Africa. Plant-It 2000 notes that the organization's goals place quality above quantity (though it mentions its total of five hundred thousand trees planted since 1992) and invokes a long list of benefits that trees provide. That list, part of the organization's Website, cites among its sources the Forest Service, the National Arbor Day Foundation, and Global ReLeaf.[48]

Slightly more expensive, and less utilitarian, is the Redwood League, through which one can have a redwood tree planted in California's Humboldt Redwoods State Park for fifty dollars. Another group, Trees For Life, is a Wichita-based organization that works in two directions simultaneously. Donations are used to plant fruit trees in developing countries (the group assigns a specific list of benefits to that goal), and the donor receives a packet with tree seeds for planting locally (i.e., in the United States), particularly with a child. For twenty-five dollars you get seeds and "a certificate stating that 25 fruit trees have been planted in the name of your child in developing countries around the world. You get to experience the miracle of your child and a tree growing up together. And the world gets fruit trees that provide food for hungry people and protect the environment. That's planting hope."[49]

While groups like these must compete for support among the general public, they can also partner with organizations such as American Forests and seek grants from government at a variety of levels. To do so, they must conform to certain standards, yet there is still an enormous range of tree planters, addressing the landscape in many locations, who cater to particular interests and advance the cause of specific groups. These proliferating groups have cluttered the arena, provoking some of the established groups to deride the fly-by-night opportunists they see cashing in on the popularity of planting and its ability to elicit donations. Though the marginal groups contribute to the proliferation of the planting discourse, only the more mainstream organizations qualify for government and timber industry support.

THE NATIONAL TREE TRUST

One funding source, created specifically to promote partnerships and sponsor local tree planting groups, is the National Tree Trust, an outgrowth of the America the Beautiful Act initiated in 1990 during the George H. W. Bush administration. Initial funding for the trust—which now operates as a 501c(3) nonprofit organization—came from a onetime congressional allocation of 20 million dollars. The trust "mobilizes volunteer groups, promotes public awareness, provides grants, and unites civic and corporate institutions in support of local tree planting and education projects."[50] Its purpose, as outlined in the America the Beautiful Act of 1990, is to

1. Promote public awareness and volunteerism in support of community tree planting
2. Solicit and accept private sector contributions for community tree planting
3. Administer private gifts and make grants for community tree planting
4. Ensure the legacy of "America the Beautiful"[51]

Planting groups can apply to various National Tree Trust programs for planting stock or financial support for a range of activities, and the trust emphasizes the partnership aspect of the work in its public relations efforts as it channels funds from the timber industry and other corporate interests to the local groups that do the planting. The National Tree Trust's primary donor of funds has been Texaco, but the organization has enjoyed a close relationship with major timber and paper product companies as well. The how-to handbook distributed to each group receiving support from the trust has sample press releases for use in promoting local planting projects. The model text reads in part:

> Trees for the National Tree Trust's projects are grown at the nurseries of 13 forest product industry companies who have partnered with the National Tree Trust since 1991. The National Tree Trust's 13 donating sponsors are: Champion International Corporation; Georgia-Pacific Corporation; International Paper; Kimberly-Clark Corporation; Louisiana-Pacific Corporation; The Mead Corporation; Mill Creek Farm; Potlatch Corporation; Simpson Timber Company; Temple-Inland Corporation; U.S. Alliance Coosa Pines Corporation; Westvaco Corporation; and Weyerhaeuser Company.[52]

The National Tree Trust's reach in the media is impressive: the organization's 1999 annual report notes that it was mentioned in "309 print news media clippings, reaching a minimum circulation of 12,835,166 people across the country," as well as in a number of national magazines.[53] In each, the timber industry's support of local activities is mentioned prominently. And even more overtly than the National Arbor Day Foundation or American Forests, the National Tree Trust wraps itself in the mantle of patriotism, given that it was born of the "America the Beautiful" program, is headed by a retired Marine Corps general, and is committed to "planting America's future." Its board of directors represents a cross section of the tree planting community, with Andy Lipkis of TreePeople sitting alongside heads of major timber corporations. By supporting groups such as TreePeople, the trust can reach out to millions of Americans with the tree planting message. Without the support of the timber industry, however, the trust would have little beyond the message to offer. By acting as a conduit, it has both the outreach and the financial inducement to gain subscribers to its program and methods. In essence, the trust's sponsors pay for the program, and in return they are able to influence the message, and be a visible part of it through public recognition of their generosity.

BAITING THE HEGEMONIC HOOK

Government in the United States, and particularly the federal government, has a defining role in promoting tree planting by the general public. Through the hierarchy of agency support outlined here—that is, federal, state, and local—the government provides money, information,
expertise, and material for outreach. This package of support is issued
directly by the government and indirectly through the nonprofit tree
planting organizations that exist in thousands of communities. The government, and particularly the Forest Service, partners with flagship
groups like the National Arbor Day Foundation and American Forests,
but it also contributes to the small local groups throughout the country
that connect with residents. By doing so, it extends the influence of a relatively small amount of money by coupling it with a focused and powerful message.

The government sets the tone from the top, and the grassroots organizations do much of the work. Though the local activists and general public have their own motivations for planting trees, and their own attach-
ment to trees, the system of support incorporates them within a common
sphere. Tree City USA, for instance, is a National Arbor Day Foundation
program, but it is facilitated by state foresters on budgets provided at
least in part by the Forest Service. To qualify for Tree City USA status, a
municipality must comply with a set of criteria furnished by the foundation and be evaluated by the state. This produces a certain uniformity in
both mission and message.

A similar dynamic is at work in the National Tree Trust and its funding program: the money it offers is contingent on meeting certain conditions and sharing a common purpose. Cooperation with a government
agency is not mandatory, of course, but financial and technical support is
seductive. What is more, the competition among tree planting groups,
and between such groups and other green causes, can make governmental support an important element in organizational viability. Tree planting organizations are subject to the pressures of competition with other
nongovernmental organizations and must find a way to enlist and maintain loyal supporters.

In the contest for stature and influence, government support can be a critical factor. The Forest Service distributes the brochures of the National Arbor Day Foundation and helps sponsor the conferences of American Forests. At the same time, the message put forth by the government— that tree planting is an important act that can shape the environment and improve nature—serves the purposes of these organizations, as they are channels for citizen participation in a communal act of stewardship. Mutual benefit is the element that enlists the institutions of civil society in a hegemonic role, and, for the government, the tree planting organizations are a solid and cheap investment. They require little funding— particularly when the timber industry is willing to help foot the bill— but extend the outreach of the government in ways that the federal bureaucracy, on its own, cannot.

Hegemony is the counterpoint of force: it operates through enlistment, persuasion, and cooptation and by conveying a sense of partnership in a common enterprise. That sense of community is clearly and, I believe, sincerely felt by those engaged in tree planting, whether they be staffers for the Forest Service's Urban and Community Forestry Programs, state forestry officials, municipal tree planters, or members of nonprofit planting groups of any size. How government and capital interests gain from this concept, and the role of the timber industry in fashioning it, is explored further in chapter 6.

SIX The Greatest Good

Reforestation is a rising giant on the American land.

James Stevens, 1950

Forestry in the United States since the beginning of the twentieth century has been a dialectic between the Forest Service and the timber
industry; at times the relationship has been more collegial, at times
more adversarial, and often it has been some combination of the two.
The subject of this chapter is tree planting as carried out for and depicted
by the timber industry; but in order to understand these activities, it is
necessary to examine first the relationship between the industry and the
government—both direct and indirect. The previous chapter discussed
the ways that government supports nonprofit tree planting; however,
most of the government's direct involvement with the nation's forests
concerns production and conservation in the national forest system. By
regulating and promoting harvesting on private land, the government is
also a critical player in the fortunes of the timber industry.

Understanding the issues surrounding the commercial use of the forests—the process of turning trees into timber, paper, and other products—is critical to understanding how and why the timber industry talks about planting trees. Following an examination of the Forest Service's role in tree planting, I turn to the timber industry and explore its activities on private land and its contribution to the mythology surrounding trees and the environment. The partnership of government and capital interests is a key element of the hegemonic discourse, and it provides a vehicle for advancing the ideas about tree planting that the two share with the nonprofit planters.

EARLY GOALS OF THE FOREST SERVICE

The United States has a long history of promoting tree planting, but the rise of the Forest Service stemmed from concern for existing forests. In the late nineteenth and early twentieth centuries, rapid consumption of the country's forests gave rise to a conservation ethic, and in 1891 the Creative Act authorized the establishment of forest reserves. The Organic Act of 1897 stipulated how such reserves would be used and protected, placing them under the authority of the Department of the Interior. In the following year, Gifford Pinchot became chief of the Forestry Division, initiating a tenure lasting from 1898 to 1910 that shaped what would become, in 1905, the Forest Service.

Pinchot was a close ally of Teddy Roosevelt, and the pair set out to put large swaths of the country under federal control. Their goal was to regulate the use of the land, and their ethic was a mix of both conservation and preservation. Pinchot viewed the timber industry with some suspicion, but he also advocated use of the national forests as a source for raw materials, most obviously wood. Pinchot is widely, but incorrectly, credited with coining the phrase he used to describe the mission of the nation's forests: "to serve the greatest good of the greatest number in the long run."[1] His interpretation of this dictum included the application of government oversight on both public and private land, and the latter portion of this regulatory orientation put him at odds with private timberland owners large and small. Pinchot eventually parted ways with the government—and ultimately with the American Forests organization as well—over his insistence that private landowners should not be allowed to manage the land without close government oversight.

Despite Pinchot's mistrust of the timber industry, the government was not in the business of processing and marketing wood and paper products; it could act only as an agent for the sale of the trees in the national forests. This necessitated a relationship between the Forest Service, as managers of the land, and the timber companies, as purchasers of the right to cut and take the trees growing on the land. Having a dual role as regulator-conserver and guardian of the public trust, on the one hand, and grower-supplier and agent of big business on the other, created tension within and concerning the Forest Service that still exists today. At times, there is a conflict of interest that relates both to the internal functioning of the agency and to its mission on behalf of the general public. Evidence of the supply/conserve conundrum that faces the Forest Service, and that is in part created by it, can be found in the evolution of its policies and in the lawsuits that serve as the signposts of its recent history. While the lawsuits relate primarily to the cutting of the forests and the effects on associated flora, fauna, and watersheds, the planting activities of the Forest Service have often been set in motion by congressional responses to the diminution in the forests that comes from that cutting.

THE GROWTH OF FEDERAL TREE PLANTING

A major step in the development of the Forest Service as a tree planting agency was the Clarke-McNary Act of 1924.[2] Increasingly, those concerned about the nation's forests were warning that the country's timber supply might, in fact, be exhaustible. An editorial in the American Forests journal reported that "in order to balance forest growth and forest consumption[,] we must restore to full production 81,000,000 acres of denuded lands . . . and 250,000,000 acres of second-growth lands[,] most of which are producing only a fraction of what they might. We must also cut our remaining 138,000,000 acres of virgin forest so that they will be replaced by fully stocked stands of desirable species."[3]

Such draconian positions created a climate that fostered passage of the Clarke-McNary Act, which grew out of a congressional report that surveyed the health of the forests and advocated a more aggressive approach to maintaining them or restoring them to economic viability. The Act had the strong support of American Forests and William B. Greeley, then chief of the Forest Service. Greeley's approach to private landowners and industry was quite different from that of Pinchot, and during Greeley's tenure as chief (1920–1928) the Forest Service "evolved into a management arm" of the timber industry.[4] The Clarke-McNary Act was grounded in a spirit of cooperation and legislated an expanded role for the government on federal lands combined with assistance for private landowners. It funded tree planting on public land, which put the Forest Service into the business of planting new stock on areas that had been cut or burned.

In addition, the Act funded efforts to suppress fires and fight disease and pests in the forests, a package seen as providing incentive for private landowners to reforest or afforest their lands. Federal money was also allocated to develop state forest nurseries, fund local educational extension work, and pay tax benefits that would stimulate timber growing. A tax study by a specialist at Yale University was commissioned to assess ways to encourage long-term investment in forestland, though, at the time, forest owners often avoided the tax burden entirely.[5] Several years after the passage of the Clarke-McNary Act, Greeley retired from the Forest Service and took a position with the West Coast Lumberman's Association, a move that confirmed for some critics that the agency was in the service of timber barons rather than the public. Pinchot commented that Greeley's tenure as chief of the Forest Service was "pitiful";[6] in the long term, it was Greeley's protimber orientation that dominated the agency and the government in general. Indeed, under Greeley the agency had made a rapid transition from implementing a vision of conservation and preservation to facilitating a more orderly yet still ambitious timber harvest.

The next significant step in the path to federal tree planting was the Knutson-Vandenberg Act of 1930,[7] which came on the heels of the economic boom of the 1920s. K-V, as it is called in the Forest Service, created a special fund dedicated to reforesting land in the national forests. The mechanism operated as a percentage of timber sales: when a company won a bid to cut timber on national forest land, it was assessed an additional fee to cover reforesting the land after the harvest. The intent of the Act was to link the money generated by a timber sale to replanting that specific site, but over the years, K-V has taken on a dynamic that often defeats this original goal.

As the needs of the national forest system grew more complex—and expensive—an administrative ruling within the Forest Service allowed K-V funds to be diverted for other purposes, including fire fighting. This fit within the Forest Service's interpretation of how to achieve its mandate to provide a continuous supply of timber, but the diversion of K-V money has been criticized on a number of grounds.[8] The reallocation has been challenged in court as being an illegal circumvention of Congress, as it takes a significant amount of the K-V fund—up to one-third by some estimates—and uses it for administrative purposes that do not improve the forestland following timber cutting. K-V is characterized by some Forest Service employees as a "boondoggle that fuels a bloated Forest Service bureaucracy . . . and creates an incentive to log no matter the environmental or fiscal costs."[9] In many respects, K-V became an adjunct of the moneymaking apparatus that creates a partnership between the Forest Service and the timber industry.[10]

Richard Moulton, head tree counter for the Forest Service (now retired), posits three major peaks in federal tree planting. He associates them with the work of the Civilian Conservation Corps, which began during the depression and continued through World War II; the Soil Bank Program, from 1956 to 1961; and the Conservation Reserve Program of the 1980s. Each of these programs led to the planting of over 2 million *acres* of trees, a figure that dwarfs the planting done on the lands of the national forests.[11] In fact, there has been long-standing concern in the Forest Service and elsewhere about a backlog of reforestation projects; in any given year, there is considerably more land slated for reforestation

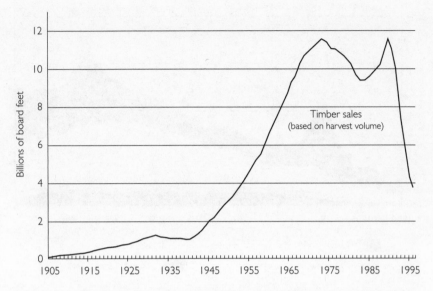

Figure 16.   Timber harvests from national forests, 1905–1996. Source: USDA Forest Service, 2001.

than is actually planted. This has contributed to the complaints about the diversion of K-V money from planting activities that has helped to maintain the backlog.

In 1990, the number of national forest acres needing reforestation stood at 1,224,804, and in that year 498,300 acres were planted. In 1999, the Forest Service replanted 268,520 acres of land, out of a total 678,769 acres awaiting forestation.[12] The decrease related in large measure to declining harvests in the national forests, indicated in figure 16. With less cutting there was less to replant, but at the same time, there was also less K-V money available to pay for the reforestation needed. This downturn came after an extended period of increased planting that followed World War II, and it mirrors a similar decrease in planting on private land following the historic peaks of the 1980s (see fig. 17). The upturn in planting on private land during the latter half of the 1990s reflects not only the diminished harvest on public land but also a shift in timber production from the Pacific Northwest—where environmental concerns have lim-

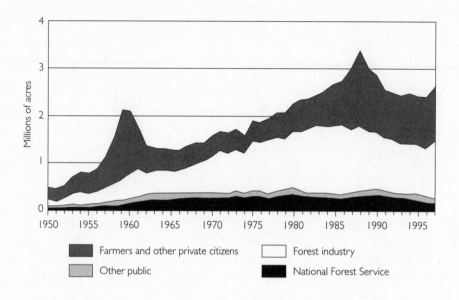

Figure 17.   Trends in reforestation, 1950–1997, in millions of acres. Source: USDA Forest Service, 2000.

ited the cut to some degree—to the south, where the industry is in a period of extended expansion.

The Forest Service has a complicated mission, traversing a minefield of politics, science, and nature with a poor map and constantly shifting terrain. The concept of sustainable use is older than the Forest Service itself and has, at least nominally, been a guiding principle throughout the agency's history. The agency's primary *function*, however, has been to sell timber and generate the next crop of merchantable trees. With the passage of the National Forests Management Act in 1976, the agency was bound to manage its land in such a way as to "preserve and enhance the diversity of plant and animal communities so that it is at least as great as that which would be expected in a natural forest."[13] Increasingly the Forest Service has had to negotiate with diverse constituencies that compete for the use or disposition of the national forests, and, since passage of the National Forests Management Act, accept the role of litigation in imposing the will of environmental advocates through the judiciary.

As a result, the timber industry is now only one of several partners to the Forest Service, and the competition to control the national forests is intense. By managing the forests for "multiple use"—that is, by serving the needs of timber supply, watershed protection, recreation, wildlife protection, and so on—the Forest Service is technically just where it was at its inception. To some extent, the battleground continues to be influenced by the chief of the Forest Service, a political appointee both subject to the whims of the White House and vulnerable to the interest-group politics that influence Congress's allocation of funds to the agency.

Many critics inside and outside the Forest Service feel that the priority of the foresters, as well as the ethos of the agency and the criteria for advancement, is to "get the cut out." Though the point is open to debate, and though the Forest Service is experiencing a generational shift and much internal dissent, it is still in the business of growing and selling trees for timber production, and still a partner to the forest products industries. In order to justify harvesting timber in the forests, the Forest Service has to argue that tree planting can replace the trees taken, and that the land can be successfully managed for diverse needs while experiencing an ongoing cycle of destruction and "rebirth." The revealing slogan of the agency's national forest management staff is: "Our job is growing."[14] And according to the rosy outlook offered by another Forest Service slogan, "There will always be forests for future generations."[15]

This attitude is certainly shared by the timber industry, and at times it is difficult to delineate exactly where the government ends and the timber industry begins. An exhibit space in the main lobby of the Forest Service building in Washington, D.C., is partly filled by a display titled *Uses of Wood*. On a visit there, I picked up a pamphlet from a table next to the display. It notes that "forests in the United States are growing far more wood than people are using every day." It also states, "Wood is made by trees using 100% solar energy. Trees take carbon dioxide out of the atmosphere and release oxygen." Further, it advises the reader that, "like the farmer who raises corn, the forest owners and wood producers are served by the U.S. Department of Agriculture, through the Forest

Service."[16] This comparison of forests to corn farming is a telling one, and, as it happens, this pamphlet distributed in the lobby of the Forest Service is issued by the Maine Wood Products Association, one of the agency's many timber-industry partners.

EARLY CONCERNS ABOUT IMAGE

The timber industry in the United States has often had to contend with an unfavorable image, one that depicts it as a predatory and rapacious enemy of the land and destroyer of nature. As discussed above, the Forest Service has had a complex relationship with the industry, and the creation of the national forests was a response to the industry's cut-and-run practices of the late nineteenth and early twentieth centuries, and an attempt to insure a perpetual supply of wood for the country. However, despite favorable policies and a sympathetic Forest Service, the industry viewed government involvement in forest management as an obstacle rather than an opportunity. Simultaneously, it appreciated the need to cultivate public—and thereby political—support in order to increase industry influence in Washington and the state capitals. The effort to generate a positive public image remains one of the central concerns of the timber industry today: it is a critical element of its use of the tree planting discourse in particular and of its effort to define stewardship of the forests more generally.

One of the pioneers in this image-crafting was the Weyerhaeuser Company, which in the early 1940s turned to the concept of a tree farm in order to manage its image. The phrase *tree farm* was proposed by a Weyerhaeuser public relations employee, and it was intended to "destroy the unhappy prejudices that had arisen in some quarters against [the timber] industry."[17] As the company would frame it, the tree farms made the slogan "Timber is a Crop" into a reality, since "trees are like wheat, watermelons, peanuts, persimmons, cabbage, corn, garlic, and grapes. Plant trees properly, manage the crop in a scientific manner, and regular harvests of a valuable raw material will be available for just as long as the cycle is continued."[18] According to Weyerhaeuser, that meant that trees

Figure 18. In a 1946 image, Weyerhaeuser portrays a "perpetual harvest" in an early attempt to depict timber harvesting as natural and the company as a responsible steward.

could be planted and harvested in perpetuity, and it was this message that the company sought to put forward.

That effort was evident in the new nomenclature of the "tree farm," but in many other ways as well. Public relations was considered a major management issue by Weyerhaeuser and other timber companies, and advertisements sought to convey the cycle of harvest and planting as the best application of science and stewardship for the land. An example of this is Weyerhaeuser's tree farm advertisement from a 1946 edition of American Forests' journal. Under the headline "Harvesting Plans for the Next 100 Years," the text describes plans for the company's Mount Saint Helens operations (see fig. 18). The caption reads, "This animated map illustrates the cyclical progression of the perpetual harvest. Its factual background rests on unembellished work-a-day maps, plans, estimates, analyses and volumes of detailed supporting data."[19] The signs on the map identify the stages in the timber production cycle of the forest, with phrases such as "Hands off until 2010 A.D.," "Then the Cycle Begins All Over Again," "Old Seed Trees," "Young Forests Growing Here," and the somewhat puzzling "This Area Reserved for Emergencies Only."

In addition to targeting specialized outlets like *American Forests* and the journal of the Society of American Foresters, Weyerhaeuser's public outreach over the succeeding decades included advertisements in popular magazines such as *Look, Time, Atlantic, Harper's,* and the *Saturday Review,* and local newspapers as well. One such advertisement, placed in both the *Saturday Evening Post* and *Time* in September and November of 1963, offers a "Guide to the Weyerhaeuser Woods." It describes a "never-ending cycle" of growth and harvest and suggests that "private industry's reforestation programs include prompt reseeding of cut-over land[,] . . . insuring a good start on fresh new growth."[20] Its own in-house newsletter, *Weyerhaeuser News,* notes with pride that the advertisement reached 10 million readers via those two magazine editions alone.[21]

REINVENTING THE FOREST INDUSTRY

The timber industry has a history of being attentive to environmental aspects of public relations. Yet despite prodigious efforts, the image of the timber industry has remained much as it always has been in the eyes of the general public—that is, hostile to the environment. In an era of increasing governmental oversight, and with the groundswell of environmental sentiment that came with the Earth Day era, it became even more important for the industry to fashion an image that would earn it support rather than opprobrium. The obvious alternative to being an enemy of the environment is to be a friend of the environment. The industry began to move in that direction, at least in terms of its public relations efforts, a tactic designed to restore or preserve the industry's influence on forest policy.

The timber consultant and author Jean Mater suggests, "The forest industry will regain the opportunity to be stewards of the forest only if it wins the public's confidence. Education and public relations have failed in this mission. Regaining stature will come through *Reinventing the Forest Industry* [the title of one of Mater's books]. When the forest industry is trusted not to 'spoil' or 'devastate' the forests, it will put a new spin on the image of the forest industry."[22] Though in principle the law says that the timber industry must abide by many state and federal regulations, the industry also has a great degree of latitude in how it manages private forestland. Thus the suggestion that timber corporations currently do not have the "opportunity to be stewards of the forest" bespeaks an ambition to have less government regulation and even more freedom in managing the forests, a sentiment that echoes throughout the natural-resource extraction world. Mater goes on to propose, "One solution is for businesses to attempt to create an image of responsibility by using sophisticated advertisements. Programs like planting a tree in a customer's honor aim to develop the image of environmental responsibility."[23] As the industry would have it, the "customer" is the general public, trees are planted in our (the country's) honor, and therefore timber companies properly distinguish themselves as environmental stewards. This argument is constructed mainly on the premise that trees can be harvested and new ones planted endlessly, that through industrial forestry the forest itself can be improved and the environment maintained or even enhanced. The timber industry has a lot to say in the public tree planting discourse, which becomes evident in an examination of their programs and public relations material.

THE SUSTAINABLE FORESTRY INITIATIVE

To influence and improve the industry's forest practices and create a mechanism for publicizing its environmental policies, the main trade association, the American Forest and Paper Association, developed a voluntary program, the Sustainable Forestry Initiative. Created in 1994, the initiative is a set of standards that address forestland management, and a mechanism for certifying compliance with those standards. Though the

Sustainable Forestry Initiative is a voluntary program, it has generated significant peer pressure among the leaders in the industry, and participation has grown rapidly. By 1999, its standards had been adopted by 152 companies "representing approximately 84% of paper production, 50% of solid wood production, and 90% of industrial timberland in the United States."[24]

The Sustainable Forestry Initiative is operated by the American Forest and Paper Association but has its own board of directors, made up of members from different interest groups. The composition of the board mirrors that of the nonprofit planting groups and of government committees such as the National Urban and Community Forestry Advisory Council, though it is weighted more heavily with members of the timber industry. Board members include the executive director of the Society of American Foresters; the chief executive officers of the Georgia-Pacific, Plum Creek, Willamette, International Paper, and Simpson timber companies; the state forester of Minnesota; the dean of the College of Forest Resources at the University of Washington; nonindustrial private forest owners; the executive director of the Izaak Walton League; the senior vice president of the Conservation Fund; and the chief executive officer of Conservation International.[25]

Assisting the board of the Sustainable Forestry Initiative is the Expert Review Panel, which comments on the program's guidelines and monitoring practices. The Expert Review Panel includes several state foresters, a number of academics (at one time, James Fazio of the University of Idaho, who writes for the National Arbor Day Foundation and who was a member of the board of directors of the National Urban and Community Forestry Advisory Council, was on the panel), members of the Forest Service and the Environmental Protection Agency, representatives from conservation organizations, and Neil Sampson, who is executive secretary of the review panel while also head of the Sampson Group forestry and natural resources consultants and former executive director and current senior fellow of American Forests. The review panel is assisted in its work by the research of the Sustainable Forestry Initiative's Forest Monitoring Project, which generates data on aspects of forestry relevant to the program's interests. The fact of the oversight review panel, and the initiative's apparent use of science, adds credibility to the initiative. This is a critical issue for a program that originates within the industry and is presented as a mechanism of self-regulation preferable to close government oversight. To show that the Sustainable Forestry Initiative has teeth, program materials often report the number of participants that have been expelled (sixteen in 2001) or suspended (twenty-two that year) for noncompliance.

In one of its brochures, the American Forest and Paper Association says, "The Sustainable Forestry Initiative suggests a dramatic departure from normal approaches to managing our natural resources," and that many "forest and paper companies have followed some of these Forestry Principles [in the past], but no company has followed all of them."[26] This statement is not accompanied by an explanation, but it appears that "normal" could mean unsustainable; thus the new "sustainable" practices could be a dramatic departure, even though the timber industry claimed sustainability long before the term's use in popular vernacular and scientific scrutiny gave it its current value. It is also unclear who the "our" in the statement refers to. One of the principles of the Initiative is to "protect the ability of all private landowners to manage their forestland in a sustainable manner,"[27] suggesting that "our" refers to the timber industry. Indeed, "American Forest & Paper Association members will support efforts to protect private property rights."[28] In the debates over land use and natural resources, the phrase *private property rights* is generally associated with an antiregulatory and antienvironmentalist stance. Yet, at the same time, the Sustainable Forestry Initiative claims to be about providing resources for all Americans, and for future generations, thus "our natural resources," in that sense, positions initiative members as stewards of a common good. In this regard, its authors try to portray the timber industry as engaged in serving the greatest good of the greatest number in the long run.

THE INITIATIVE'S FORESTRY GOALS

The Sustainable Forestry Initiative approaches stewardship of forestlands by pursuing several objectives that form the criteria for certification of its members. Its first stated objective is to "broaden the practice of sustainable forestry by employing an array of scientifically, environmentally, and economically sound practices in the growth, harvest, and use of forests." The second objective is slightly more specific though still vague: "ensure long-term forest productivity and conservation of forest resources through prompt reforestation, soil conservation, afforestation and other measures."[29] The details of how to achieve these goals come in the implementation and verification guidelines, which are specific; in material intended for the media and the general public, however, the objectives remain platitudinous and general. The third through tenth initiative objectives are, in brief form, as follows:

- Protect water quality
- Enhance wildlife habitat
- Minimize the visual impact of clear-cutting
- Protect land with particular ecologic, geologic, or historic significance
- Contribute to biodiversity
- Help ensure the efficient use of forest resources
- Promote cooperation between forestry sectors and owners to support sustainability
- Report to the public on members' progress in meeting the initiative's goals

According to the eleventh objective, the initiative's goal is to "provide opportunities for the public and the forestry community to participate in the commitment to sustainable forestry,"[30] which entails, in no small measure, helping them to consume information about what the timber industry is doing on behalf of the public. The Sustainable Forestry Initiative has become the touchstone for timber industry public relations, and participation is offered as proof of a company's environmental virtue and of that of the industry as a whole. Along with the Sustainable Forestry Initiative campaign, publicity about individual facets of stewardship and about the programs of particular companies continues to draw attention to the value of trees and the environmental benevolence of the industry.

TREE PLANTING WRIT LARGE

Several themes and issues stand out in the timber industry's chronicle of tree planting activities. The most pronounced is that the industry plants a prodigious number of trees every year, and that timber stock is increasing in the United States. The upshot, offered in a variety of industry slogans and programs, is that the process of extraction is sustainable, and that "America Will Never Grow Out of Trees." Next in the list of claims is that the industry's tree planting is beneficial for the environment—that is, appropriate trees, planted in the right way, provide myriad benefits for local and global ecosystems. The idea is that the industry is "improving tomorrow's environment today."[31] Finally, the timber industry presents itself as a responsible and generous supporter of all those who, like itself, are engaged in making the world a better place for consumers, other creatures, and the forest.

Individual timber companies and the American Forest and Paper Association represent their tree planting as a massive effort; at the same time, they characterize the benefits as being available to each person. They marshal statistics from particular companies or holdings and from the industry as a whole; the aggregate tree planting figures, and interpretations of their significance, frequently issued by the association, are cited widely by companies and the government. One of the more modest numerical claims concerns the number of trees planted annually by the industry. It is published in a brochure titled "A Tree for Each American," which shows an abstracted American flag superimposed over a bright green forest scene. It backs the "for Each American" claim with numbers showing how many trees each person consumes per year and in what forms, and how many are planted—one for each American. The brochure assures readers that, despite the impressive list of types and amounts of consumption, "we still have about two-thirds of the forest cover that existed in the 1600s. And more forest cover than existed in 1900."[32] In this way, the public can be proud and feel patriotic about the consumption of trees, inasmuch as the total forest, under the stewardship of the timber industry, is said to be increasing.

The numbers are repeated in various forms, and with great regularity in the American Forest and Paper Association's publications. In *Healthy Forests for a Healthy Environment*, for example, the association states, "In fact, we have more trees today than we had 70 years ago. And some 4 million more are planted each day."[33] In this pamphlet, the association has increased the number of trees planted per capita to "more than five new trees a year for every man, woman, and child in America."[34] In its brochure *Best Management Practices to Protect Water Quality*, the annual figure is "180 trees for every child born in America."[35]

The tendency to tie these trees to individual citizens is popular in the timber industry, and the pro-timber nonprofit organization the Yellow Ribbon Coalition operates a flatbed trailer that tours the country to display forest products at schools, sporting events, and other public gatherings. Beneath a banner bearing the slogan "Forest Products from Pacific Northwest Families to Your Family," the truck has a second banner reading, "We plant six trees for every one harvested—our forests are forever."[36] The Timber Employees Association for Responsible Solutions, another such group, published a typical example of the numbers fetish—albeit with an unusual mathematical twist—as an advertisement in *The Oregonian* newspaper in 1990. Under the headline "Endangered Forests?" it noted, "In 1989[,] 130 million trees were planted—6 trees for every American."[37]

The reported ratios of trees or acres planted to population size, and aggregated or disaggregated numbers of trees for the industry as a whole or for a particular company, are simultaneously impressive and, for most people, relatively meaningless. In comparative terms, the ten trees that the National Arbor Day Foundation member receives, or even the millions that American Forests has set as a goal, pale beside the number of trees planted by the timber industry, making industry efforts appear monumental. These numbers, however—both the millions of Global ReLeaf trees and the tens or hundreds of millions, or billions, of the timber industry—can be little more than an abstraction for most people, as their knowledge of forests, trees, and even the meaning of an acre is poorly developed.

PLANTING FOR WILDLIFE AND DIVERSITY

An additional component of the timber industry's effort to educate the public is its representation of the diversity of the trees that it plants in such massive numbers. In describing the types of trees that it plants, the industry is responding to charges that it creates monoculture plantations (i.e., tree farms), which are artificial, fail to support a diverse ecosystem, are particularly vulnerable to pests and disease, and deprive wildlife of critical habitats. The fourth objective of the Sustainable Forestry Initiative, stated in full, is: "Enhance the quality of wildlife habitat by developing and implementing measures that promote habitat diversity and the conservation of plant and animal populations found in forest communities."[38]

While such measures may at times be voluntary, this objective also reflects the reality of legal restrictions and challenges to business-as-usual forestry in the era of the Endangered Species Act and the northern spotted owl controversy. Rather than setting a particular standard that would apply across all forestlands, the performance measures contained in the Sustainable Forestry Initiative's fourth objective are worded to allow members to adjust to or accommodate local necessities. Section (a) of those measures says, "Each American Forest & Paper Association member company will define its own policies, programs, and plans to promote habitat diversity."[39] In one of its publications, titled "Answers to Some Frequently Asked Questions," the association asks, "Doesn't it harm wildlife when trees are cut down?" and it answers, "A managed forest . . . provides the greatest variety of habitats for the greatest diversity of wildlife species."[40] Though the forest may provide the habitat, the timber industry intensively manages its land and the ecosystems both on and in it, keeping close tabs on the living creatures that exist there. International Paper, for example,

> recognizes the existence of threatened and endangered plants and animals as part of the landscape. We work with groups such as the U.S. Fish and Wildlife Service, numerous state heritage groups, state fish and wildlife agencies, and The Nature Conservancy to identify and manage these species. Accurate inventories are maintained for species that occur on

company lands because we work as land stewards to conserve these species and their habitat. To date, 12 threatened or endangered species have been identified on our lands. Management plans are developed and implemented for individual species.[41]

Again, the language is instructive, as the endangered species are recognized as "part of the landscape"—that is, as subjects of stewardship on land that *belongs* to International Paper, rather than as creatures living on land that is *used* by International Paper. Timber companies create habitat conservation plans that dovetail with their timber harvest and generation plans, with profit being at least partly contingent on accommodating externally mandated environmental concerns. In a brochure, the Boise Cascade Corporation notes that "you can harvest timber to meet society's needs and protect fish and wildlife habitat at the same time," though elsewhere it expresses a measure of hostility to the Endangered Species Act.[42] After a harvest, of course, trees must grow back; this is the premise of the "renewable resource" that America will never grow short of. Thus, after cutting its timber, Weyerhaeuser plants

> trees that are native to the area. In the South, we plant primarily loblolly pine, which is the dominant natural species. In some areas we also plant oaks, sweet gum, bald cypress, ash and yellow poplar. In the Northwest, we plant primarily Douglas-fir, and also plant noble fir, hemlock, ponderosa pine, cedar, red alder and other indigenous species[,] depending on soil, elevation and climatic conditions. Even in areas where we plant predominantly one species, our forests are far from being a "monoculture." Shrubs, ferns, grasses and other "wild" species of both hardwood and softwood trees—brought in from surrounding areas by the wind or birds—grow among our planted trees.[43]

Thus, whether the plants and trees have been deliberately placed on the land or have grown from seeds blown in from elsewhere, "as vegetation covers the land, insects, animals and birds follow."[44]

Again, according to Weyerhaeuser, the issue of biological diversity has in recent years received "widespread public attention as it evolved from concern over remote tropical forests—to temperate and tropical forests the world over."[45] In order to address such concerns, the timber industry

generates a wealth of material that publicizes its efforts to promote, conserve, and even improve the conditions that support flora and fauna on
the land it uses to generate timber. Though the tree farm concept is still
in use both practically and rhetorically, timber companies are quick to
speak about their "forests" and to argue that they are "continuously look-
ing for better ways to improve the health and productivity" of those
forests.[46] The claims to stewardship can be quite broad-ranging and even
include the statement by Georgia-Pacific declaring, "Clearcutting the forest: it's nature's way."[47] While the timber industry promotes itself as a
champion of biological diversity and steward of wildlife—the Plum
Creek Corporation calls itself "the environmental leader"[48]—it reminds
the public as well that it is simultaneously a provider for human consumers.

One tool that timber companies use to carry out their mandate is the
"improved" tree. Increased yield from the forestland is a complex formula that considers the pace of growth, the quality of the trees, and the
capital investments and values tied up in bringing the forest to harvest.
Timber companies and the Forest Service dedicate considerable research
to finding varieties that resist disease, grow rapidly, and produce straight
and relatively limb-free trees that will respond to the management practices and geographies of particular companies and their forests. Particular trees, or types of trees, have become corporate property not just in
terms of their physical possession but in terms of their genetic composition as well. Weyerhaeuser has developed what it calls "Plus trees," tailored to grow the type of tree that the company desires for wood and
fiber production, while International Paper's "genetically improved
SuperTrees can grow four to five feet per year on good sites to allow a
new forest to appear in a matter of a few short years."[49] International
Paper claims that, "when planted and managed with our state-of-the-art
technologies, SuperTree seedlings can produce three to four times the
wood volume of natural forests."[50]

The suggestion that fast-growing seedlings can constitute a forest in a
few short years illustrates the superficial nature of many industry claims
concerning the environment. Though individual companies and the
American Forest and Paper Association point to the amount of money

that they invest in research, the efforts they make to "promote" wildlife and care for nature, and the land they set aside to protect sensitive habitats, these are, at most, ancillary to the business of getting maximum output from the land through intensive alteration and manipulation of—often including the destruction of—natural systems. Yet the timber industry casts itself not only as a steward but also as the expert, caring for the animals, the environment, and society better than those constituents can care for themselves.

CARBON SEQUESTRATION AND THE GLOBAL ENVIRONMENT

The timber industry proclaims itself a guardian at an even grander scale, as a defender against global climate change. As noted earlier, the concept of carbon sequestration in trees has generated widespread enthusiasm for planting individual trees and forests to favorably affect atmospheric conditions and slow the pace of global warming. International Paper took the lead in this regard and placed a number of full-page newspaper advertisements in the wake of the Kyoto Conference on global climate change. According to an ad it published in the *New York Times*, "If the world is warming, managed forests may be the best thermostat," because

> carbon dioxide is a principal contributor to the greenhouse effect. By reducing the atmosphere's carbon levels, trees help counter this effect. Young, growing trees are particularly efficient at this process. Which is where we at International Paper come in. We're the largest private owner of forestland in the United States. With over six million acres of forests, we manage one of the most potent carbon-absorbing and oxygen-supplying resources in the country. For nearly 100 years we've been responsibly managing our forests. For example, we plant an average of 50 million trees annually, far more than we harvest.[51]

International Paper's slogan "We answer to the world" is ambitious in its imagery—compare it to one of Weyerhaeuser's corporate mottos, "The Tree Planting Company." International Paper links its tree planting prowess to issues of global climate change and notes that it is "the world's largest private seedling grower."[52] This apparently adds up to a significant effect on the environment, as "the young, fast-growing seedlings we generate . . . and plant on company land are oxygen factories that use 1.47 lb. of carbon and give off 1.07 lb. of oxygen for every pound of wood they grow."[53] The Simpson Timber Company provides a formula like the ones used by American Forests and the Forest Service, noting that "an average 100 foot tree absorbs 8,000 pounds of carbon dioxide and manufactures 6,000 pounds of oxygen."[54]

Recent research has challenged the utility of tree planting in carbon sequestration, an issue discussed in chapter 7. It is interesting to note, however, that Weyerhaeuser anticipated the discussion of global warming and the role that trees might play in absorbing atmospheric carbon. The relationship was discussed in a 1968 article in the *Weyerhaeuser Newsletter* titled "Forests Contribute to the Breath of Life." The article is based on a presentation made by a Weyerhaeuser plant physiologist, John Rediske, at a meeting of the Society of American Foresters. Rediske writes, "What we are capable of doing to our environment is . . . the most critical problem facing mankind. It could be a matter of survival, and the forests of the world are closely associated with that survival."[55] The article goes on to discuss the role of trees in absorbing carbon, and the potential dangers of rapid anthropogenic emission of greenhouse gasses. Twenty years later, of course, the timber industry would be wary about accepting the global warming scenario. But, like American Forests, it would be quick to advertise its role in combating it once tree planting was popularized as a vehicle for carbon sequestration. In 1968, Rediske wrote, "We may be close to a threshold where a small increase in average temperature could produce disastrous results, such as the melting of polar ice caps with an associated rise in sea level and inundation of our major ports. We simply do not know the answers to these questions."[56]

Meanwhile, despite the reluctance of the George W. Bush administration to admit it, global warming has been confirmed; the role of trees in sequestering carbon has been questioned. Through it all, the timber industry has presented itself as being invested in and committed to the environment, though clearly it has responded to public perception and the pressure of government in crafting approaches to managing the land. In the process, the timber industry has labored to position itself as being on the "same side" as environmentalists, as sharing their concern for sound environmental policies and stewardship of natural resources. To supplement this effort, demonstrate its green qualifications, and create relationships with environmentalists, the timber industry has been generous in donating money and materials to various causes, and has been vocal about the scope and depth of this support.

THE LARGESSE OF BIG TIMBER

Previous chapters have noted financial and in-kind donations to support tree planting organizations. Timber and paper companies provide direct cash contributions, paper for publications, and seedling trees to nonprofit groups like American Forests, the National Tree Trust, and local planting organizations. The industry has also channeled its support through the Forest Service and state foresters, and through grant programs that it administers directly or via corporate foundations. In addition, timber companies often undertake or contribute to educational outreach projects that provide classroom materials for schoolteachers, a form of philanthropy with a particularly focused message. Across the spectrum of support offered by the timber industry, the message is that companies are caring for the environment on their land, and that they invite the public to join them in stewarding additional areas—indeed, the whole world.

There is an obvious reason for the timber industry to provide free seedling trees as its foremost public relations tool: it allows companies to take a tax write-off for surplus material while promoting the visceral and long-lasting image of the tree and, by extension, its donor. The tree itself is a powerful symbol, but the industry packages the donation in various ways to magnify the appearance of benevolence and capitalize on the goodwill it generates. In order to maximize the effect of their donations, companies shape the terms of their gift according to specific company guidelines. Weyerhaeuser, for instance, "has a long tradition of concern and respect for the environment and support for the communities where we do our business. That is why we offer seedlings to groups that share our high standards of environmental responsibility and our appreciation for trees as a renewable resource." One of the questions Weyerhaeuser poses in order to evaluate requests for free trees is, "What education will you provide Project participants regarding trees as a renewable resource?"[57]

Much of the corporate emphasis on companies' support for community planting activities is predicated on the number of trees provided and what those trees will do for the community. The Union Camp Corporation (subsequently purchased by International Paper in 1998) gave 10 percent of its seedlings it raised each year to "conservation organizations, schools, landowners, and other organizations."[58] Many timber companies have similar seedling giveaway programs, some targeting nonprofit planting groups, others providing trees for nonindustrial private forest owners who will, presumably, sell those trees to the timber mills in the future. Trees channeled through the National Tree Trust, which has received over 8 million trees total from ten timber companies since its inception, represents the largest number of trees donated to a single source.

The timber industry also provides financial aid, materials, and sometimes, land to a wide range of conservation organizations. Two groups that seem particularly popular with the timber industry are the Nature Conservancy and the National Wild Turkey Federation; the full list of recipients is too long to replicate here. Industry philanthropy is meted out to beneficiaries that range from national organizations to neighborhood groups, and in aggregate it amounts to tens of millions of dollars and tens of millions of trees. This investment may not be completely devoid of altruism, yet it is presented within the framework of the timber company as a benevolent citizen, sharing the profit from the (environmentally managed) land with the community. Ultimately, the message is that the industry has our best interests at heart and the resources to promote them. The profit that the industry reaps from the land, and the true impact of its forestry practices, are not part of this message of altruism.

THE BUSINESS OF TREES

The government, the timber industry, and the nonprofit planting organizations all stand to gain from the proliferation of the tree planting discourse, albeit in different ways. For the government and the industry, there is an obvious commonality of purpose, that is, to generate profit from the land. Though this creates tension between the regulator and the regulated, the evolution of management practices in the Forest Service and timber industry reveals periods of cooperation bracketing periods of controversy and adversarial relations. Their common interest in timber production creates a need for both the government and the industry to communicate with the public as advocates of their own practices. As the country has turned its attention to the environment, the rhetoric concerning sustainable forestry has proliferated, and the public has been targeted as an audience that must be persuaded to adopt a specific view about trees and the environment.

The record of judicial intervention in the policies and practices of the Forest Service in recent decades reveals an ongoing bias in the executive and legislative branches of government in favor of timber production.[59] The language of multiple use and the economics of tourism may influence the national forests more today than ever before, but the economics and politics of timber sales still drive the Forest Service, particularly in areas not subject to judicial protection and oversight. The timber industry has had to respond to changes in how public lands are managed, and to new legislative and judicial restrictions on private land, but its mandate remains to secure the greatest profit possible. The governmental-industrial timber complex justifies itself by claiming that its policies and practices are sustainable and environmentally beneficial. At a deeper level, conveyed via outreach to and through the nonprofit planting and other environmental organizations, the message is that we are and must be in control of nature, directing it for our benefit and that of all other constituents of the natural world.

In recent years, the timber industry has advanced its case concerning the environment primarily through the Sustainable Forestry Initiative. This program sets standards, enforces them, measures their success, and

seeks to improve them through ongoing calibration and broader participation. Ultimately, the industry seeks to have a seal or mark of approval
which signals to consumers that a product has been produced in accordance with initiative guidelines and, therefore, is both sustainable—
whatever that may mean—and, by extension, a more "wholesome" purchase than a comparable item that lacks the program's approval. In many
ways, the Sustainable Forestry Initiative is about marketing: the marketing of images, ideas, and practices as much as, if not more than, the marketing of products. If trees are special and environmental and green, and
if the timber industry grows more trees of better quality than anyone else
and gives so many of them away, then by logical extension it must be an
appropriate steward of the land—or so says the industry's message.

According to Derek Jumper, spokesperson for the American Forest
and Paper Association, the timber industry has "to convince the
American public that it's ok to use our wood." More than that, he hopes
that the Sustainable Forestry Initiative symbol will

> help people eliminate some of that inherent guilt in daily lives. In a
> perfect world SFI [the initiative] could get to that juncture where people
> just inherently look for the SFI symbol on a product; because they don't
> really know why it's better, nor do they really care, but they know from
> the last [i.e., next] twenty-five years because it's been hammered into
> them that SFI wood or SFI forests are somehow better or more environ-
> mentally beneficial.[60]

This sentiment—the desire for a response that is not based on the public's understanding or caring, but that is simply an ingrained, conditioned
response to the industry's presentation of itself as environmental steward—captures much of the spirit and influence of the tree planting discourse. In hegemonic terms, capital interests can hope for nothing better
than a passive and loyal public that feels good about participating in a
system created to preserve the status quo even as it purports to evolve in
partnership with the society as a whole. The manufacture of an image that
seduces the public and enlists them in a common enterprise, yet deliberately or incidentally avoids furnishing or obfuscates real information
about the issues, is what is so dangerous about a hegemonic discourse.

SEVEN Celebritrees

Every time Texaco plants a tree, we plant a seed in
their minds.

Texaco Corporation advertisement, 1995

I moved from Washington, D.C., to Eugene, Oregon, in 1996, a shift from
the capital of political capital to a capital of forest capital. Eugene is the
headquarters of the Willamette National Forest, the most productive of
the national forests, and from here I have been able to watch much of the
forestry process—the process of turning trees into products, then planting
more trees—unfold around me, from beginning to end. According to an
estimate included in Standard and Poor's industry surveys, in the years
that I have lived here, the paper and wood companies of the United
States have shipped approximately 1.8 trillion dollars worth of product.[1]
During that same period, International Paper acquired both Champion
International for a price of approximately $10 billion and the Union Camp
timber company for nearly $8 billion, Georgia-Pacific purchased Fort
James (itself a merger of James River and Fort Howard timber companies)

for $11 billion, and Weyerhaeuser purchased Canada's MacMillan-Bloedel for $2.5 billion and completed a $5 billion hostile takeover of Willamette Industries.[2] International Paper, like many of the other giant timber companies, has truly international interests; it owns 1.5 million acres of land in Brazil and nearly a million acres in New Zealand, and has "harvesting rights on government-owned timberlands in Canada."[3] Such numbers display a different aspect of the power of trees: their ability to generate enormous profits for those who reap them for commercial purposes. The profit factor and associated political power highlight the necessity to closely examine the discourse of trees.

The power of trees to affect people is sufficiently obvious and compelling that it has not remained the sole province of those with a specific interest in trees. The Exxon Mobil Corporation has cashed in with its own "Planting the Future" advertisements on the op-ed page of the *New York Times*. The corporation notes, "The Christmas season is a time when trees form a central element of holiday celebrations. . . . Christmas trees remind us of the importance of trees, both as a religious symbol and as part of nature." Out of desire to make "a better future," Exxon Mobil has "supported many initiatives, involving over 100 charities, government departments and other corporate planting in tree planting. *These efforts have resulted in the planting of over 13 million trees since 1995.*"[4]

Texaco has kept pace with its energy industry competition by placing its own advertisements proclaiming that Texaco is "doing our part for the environment," which includes sponsoring the National Urban Forest Conferences and the National Tree Trust. Under a picture of a group of children (who are perhaps five or six years old and of Asian, Latin, African, and European ethnicities, to judge by their skin color), the petroleum products company reveals its hand, and that of the planting discourse more broadly, when it says, "Every time Texaco plants a tree, we plant a seed in their minds." It is not surprising that Texaco would be attuned to the value of trees, since not only does it sponsor American Forests, but its former chief executive officer is on International Paper's board of directors. He is joined there by, among others, the current or former chief executive officers of DaimlerChryslerAG, Goodyear Tire and Rubber Company, Union Carbide Corporation, Reynolds Metals

Company, and Best Foods.[5] This is, of course, typical of the network of power that pervades big business in the United States, and it reflects the consolidation of economic power and its concentration in the hands of a small yet remarkably influential interest group. This corporate elite shares a common agenda when it comes to the economy—that is, the bigger the better, with the "free market" determining the rules of engagement. And what of a possible countervailing force to such industrial behemoths?

According to Robert Gottlieb, much of the environmental movement has become "more a cri-de-coeur than [an] agenda for action, a still unfulfilled search for some alternative way to define our social and ecological universe."[6] That such an agenda is important is something I take to be self-evident; at the same time, my work is partly an attempt to call into question what is considered self-evident. Thus I review some of the constituent issues, and the roles of trees, in both the problems and the associated prescriptions outlined in this book, knowing full well that it is far easier to identify problems than solutions, and that the desire (one I share with so many others) to find healthier ecological and social relationships will not be satisfied by my work. The magnitude of corporate power and the associated participation of the government in the forest economy is daunting. Yet hegemonic conceptions can be unraveled only if they are exposed; or more realistically, so long as they remain embedded and are not critiqued, they cannot be unraveled.

ROADS NOT TAKEN

In my effort to focus on the tree planting discourse, I have sidestepped, or dealt with in a cursory manner, several significant issues and debates. Questions about nature, for instance—what it is, what it means, and how we relate to it—have generated a rich and growing literature, yet I have not delved deeply into the nuances of this critical topic. At the same time, I have chosen the title for this book precisely because of the malleability of the concept of nature, for there are many who believe that by planting trees they are *planting nature*. In ways both superficial and profound they are right, and William Cronon's characterization of the garden tree, described in chapter 1, serves as a reminder of that important fact. At the same time, many who plant trees with the conviction that they are reproducing or improving nature remain blissfully unaware of what they seek to create and of the cost of believing that what has been changed can be easily restored. Moreover, in the tree planting discourse the implications of manipulating nature are regularly championed and almost never critically questioned, even as nature is positioned as something we must protect. The idea that nature is subject to human will, whether benign, benevolent, or rapacious, is a constant and powerful current in the discussion of trees.

I have also steered away from the scientific debate on the ecological effects of modern forestry in the United States (and the rest of the world, where the practices of United States–based companies can be even more problematic), though I have presented and situated claims about this subject made by the timber industry, the government, and the nonprofit planting organizations. In many respects such debates seem reminiscent of the disputes over the effects of smoking, with the tobacco industry fighting tooth and nail to create and interpret data to support its claim that the dangers of cigarettes were unproven and the research inconclusive. In the case of the northern spotted owl, to take a particularly prominent example, the timber industry has segued from denying the problem to contesting the size of territory required for survival and the number of owls remaining, and from there to claiming that the owls can in fact thrive in habitat created for them by new, managed forests in place of old, natural ones.

One topic on which I have more overtly signaled my skepticism is the issue of global warming and the potential for carbon sequestration through planting trees. In part, this is because I am regularly struck by the abject simplification of the issue as it is presented to the public: plant trees, store carbon, slow global warming—with the only concrete fact conveyed being that even a single tree is significant in this battle. Yet in the grand equation of emissions and sequestration, tree planting has been and will remain a relatively insignificant factor for two reasons. First, the number of trees that would have to be planted in order to significantly influence the growing accumulation of atmospheric carbon has not, will not, and probably could not be planted. Potential reforestation and afforestation for the entire planet would represent only "about 2 percent of the annual global carbon uptake by the terrestrial biosphere."[7] And, despite the call for a massive increase in tree planting that came with the Kyoto Accords, carbon emissions have continued apace, as has tree planting—that is, there has been no significant gain on the carbon sequestration front through tree planting.[8]

Perhaps as troubling as the failure to plant enough trees is the reversal now taking place on the efficacy of planting trees to sequester carbon at all. The Intergovernmental Panel on Climate Change—the reigning scientific authority on these issues—began to broadly signal this "new science" in the fall of 2000. Though the panel projects that there will be continued carbon uptake by "newly planted or regenerating forests," it also notes that carbon uptake "may gradually diminish and forest ecosystems could even become a source."[9] Recent research sponsored by the government and the timber industry has shown that, after an initial uptake of carbon, trees lack sufficient nutrients to maintain their growth in a way that constitutes a carbon sink. In fact, it now seems that planting trees may facilitate a carbon transfer from the biosphere to the atmosphere (that is, from the earth to the air): rather than being a solution, disturbing existing forests and planting new trees is part of the problem.[10]

I raised this possibility (along with the complexity of calculating tree growth and economic growth in the face of looming global climate change) in interviews I conducted with nonprofit planters and members of the timber industry, but my questions were deflected. The issue was deemed "not critical" by nonprofit tree planters because, after all, there are many other benefits from trees, so it is a "no-lose" situation.[11] I was assured by timber industry foresters and spokespersons that their companies had top-notch scientists working in their labs on these questions, and that until there were definitive answers which contraindicated current practices, their policy was to continue at full speed ahead. For its part, the U.S. government continues to push for tree planting as part of its campaign against global warming. From all three sectors—the nonprofit, commercial, and governmental planters—the message about trees, about their inherent goodness, manifold benefits, and environmental contribution, remains paramount. The discourse—and the hegemonic apparatus that profits from it—rolls on.

ROADS WELL WORN

There are important ongoing discussions on the dangers or merits of genetically altered trees, the costs and benefits of monoculture forests, and the possibility of a sustainable forestry based on removing an enormous amount and critical type of biomass from a complex system on a repetitive and increasingly short cycle.[12] Many such concerns, based on earlier scientific knowledge, were present in previous debates over forestry and the environment, reviewed in chapter 2. Indeed, the pursuit of sustainability is over a century old, and not the invention of a recently informed public, a newly responsible industry, or a more regulatory government (see fig. 19). Trees themselves have been harnessed as tools to provide for our species, and as instruments for environmental alteration, for thousands of years, and concern over the loss or fate of trees is nearly as old. This generates an interesting paradox in relation to the modern discourse of trees: over and over again, traditional wisdom about traditional concerns is being "discovered" and offered as a new solution to new problems. A study of the environmental history of the United States suggests that, for the most part, the problems have persisted and worsened, and that the "solutions" have been a combination of inadequate and untested. Still, there seems to be considerable profit in reinventing the wheel.

This leads back to a question that has driven my interest in tree planting: who profits from all of this? Obviously the timber industry, the broader economy, and the enabling politicians do, at least in the short-term. But critical attention must be focused on their partnerships with the ostensibly nonprofit organizations and with the general public. Partnership in this respect includes both active participation and the passive benefit derived from a common discourse that naturalizes and promotes the activities of participants across the planting spectrum.

The players that come after won't have any "fair greens" at all if we aren't careful. (1921)

Figure 19. The "players" that Jay N. "Ding" Darling was concerned about in his 1921 cartoon have by now joined the timber industry and the government in the planting game.

More broadly, those who subscribe to the belief that the trees they plant are a panacea—for both the ills of the environment and humans' guilt for despoiling nature—benefit as well. Their profit may be primarily emotional, though if, at the same time, they accrue other, more tangible benefits, they will be that much "richer." The emotional aspect should not be downplayed, however, even if researchers have not yet found a way to quantify it economically. However, Carolyn Merchant and others describe the many problematic dimensions of the desire to restore or recreate nature, and the powerful attraction of images of an Eden that can be created through our gardening.[13]

Among those skeptical that such "ecological restoration" is even possible is Evan Eisenberg, who warns, "If we want to dream of Eden, we had better go back to sleep."[14] Though the discourse of trees may inspire us to thoughts of an Eden created by our "own" trees, we can ill afford to sleep. Yet by manipulating human emotion—by drawing upon the profound place of trees in our many cultures—as well as science, politics, and power, the tree planting discourse can lull us, as it directs our attention to symptoms rather than causes. David Harvey notes that "the general approach to environmental problems is to intervene only 'after the event.'"[15] In the functioning of a hegemonic discourse, remedial efforts can be identified as part of the problem inasmuch as they offer palliatives that, even if helpful and appealing, ultimately abet, or at least do not address, the root causes.

FOCUS ON THE SYMPTOM

One hundred years ago, concern about the effect of timber harvesting and the fate of the country's forests (and associated systems, both human and nonhuman) was both pronounced and growing. Teddy Roosevelt, like Bill Clinton more recently, made broad pronouncements about the need to husband our resources and consider future generations. Trees and forests were often the subject of impassioned debate and were prominent in the public eye—from the classroom observance of Arbor Day to the national observance of that holiday, and in myriad other ways that trees mark daily life. Progress—in the form of legislation, regulation, land designation, and the production of knowledge through science—was on the march. One hundred years later, the debates continue to rage; forestlands are regulated, reregulated, and deregulated while being legislated and adjudicated. All the while, we have been told to plant trees.

There are modified or botanically different types of trees today that did not exist one hundred years ago, of course, and a partial list of what we plant now includes wildlife trees, shade trees, fruit trees, pulp trees, ornamental trees, habitat trees, seed trees, riparian trees, memorial trees, city trees, historic trees, champion trees, shelter belt trees, phyto-remediation trees (which break down or remove pollutants from contaminated soil), "utilitrees" (designed to minimize interference with aboveground utility wires), Plus trees (developed by Weyerhaeuser), SuperTrees (developed by International Paper), and Global ReLeaf trees. Each is assigned a particular function, or many functions, defined in relation to the human environment. And according to the Forest Service, they are "serving us" everyday. How is it, then, that after more than a century of environmental advocacy on behalf of the forests, and after more than 125 years of the American Forests organization and Arbor Day, all this advocacy is still necessary, even more so now than before?

Central to my critique is the fact that trees will not accomplish all that the planters claim in their efforts to stimulate and capitalize on planting. Trees are supposed to provide us with clean air and water, for instance, but the National Arbor Day Foundation and American Forests, while talking the environmental talk, tell us how to *offset* rather than prevent degradation of these fundamental sources of life. The government, in the form of the Environmental Protection Agency, encourages us not to feel guilty about consumption and pollution so long as we engage in remediation. And the timber industry, along with many other commercial interests, not only encourages consumption but also, in an adroit display of legerdemain, promises that sustainability means that our (or rather, their) good fortune can last forever. As versatile as trees are, it seems spurious to suggest that the fate of the environment in the new century will be markedly better than it has been in the century just passed if only we plant more of them.

Yet this is the message of the tree planting discourse. It may have been true that trees could make a profound difference during the life of Johnny Appleseed, and perhaps even during the life of J. Sterling Morton, and it is still true on a small scale today. However, the *idea* that trees can make a significant difference operates across all scales, from the transformative Global ReLeaf to the still popular story *The Man Who Planted Trees* to the effect on a home-heating bill or the size of a local elk population. These scales, when aggregated, create a powerful suggestion that, if all is not well, all can be made well. And while the tree planting discourse poses effective action as something available to anyone with a shovel or a donation, it simultaneously affirms that the government and timber industry wear the mantle of stewardship.

The discourse does this through the shared fetish of numbers—planting one tree is good, planting a billion is better—and through the weight of scientific and moral authority, which are packaged with the benefits that derive from tree planting. It also builds and sustains itself through repetition and saturation. As I have shown, many different participants promulgate the message of tree planting, and one of the goals of the government is to provide language to describe tree planting. When all of this is added up—common tools, common goals, common language, common activities, and at times, common funding—it is understandable that the public would see tree planting as a common cause. And it is a common cause, except that tree planting as now practiced is better at delivering a hegemonic world than an Edenic world.

THE PRIZE

Some say that when people set out to dominate nature, they inevitably end up dominating other people. Without arguing the point, it is safe to say that power is not distributed evenly in human societies: when people set out to dominate nature, some are themselves subject to manipulation by others. When this control is overt and repressive, it is deemed incompatible with the "life, liberty, and pursuit of happiness" clause that is part of the American ethos and enshrined as part of United States law. My goal has been to illustrate another way of controlling people, through their engagement with nature. The tree planting discourse is more subtle than an overt use of force. It speaks of inclusion and engendering a sense of capability, yet its triumphal tone and grand agenda help to mask a mechanism for concentrating power and agency in the hands of those already vested with it—that is, capital interests and the political system that responds to their needs. Ultimately, the discourse contributes to a hegemonic conception that hands nature over to those who seek to profit from its management, in spite of the obvious costs of doing so, which capital interests share far more generously with the public than the profits.

The critical element, according to Gramsci, is that the general public *willingly participates* in this system and is conditioned to do so by the institutions of civil society. In the case I discuss here, groups like the National Arbor Day Foundation, American Forests, TreePeople, and so many others provide an opportunity for people to link with government and industry in dominating the environment. Even those who oppose the practices of timber giants like International Paper or Weyerhaeuser are hard pressed to understand, let alone explain, what might be wrong with tree planting as practiced by the experts.

Even more challenging for those who oppose such practices would be to argue that cooperation between government, industry, and environmentalists can be problematic. Groups such as the National Arbor Day Foundation and American Forests suggest that positive engagement is the key to influencing the process, and that the issues must be approached in an incremental manner. While this approach may have some practical and philosophical appeal, and may in some cases be the appropriate approach, the ongoing degradation of the planet and its ecosystems makes such an orientation look like treating cancer with morphine: pain will be relieved, a measure of pleasure may even be induced, but the disease remains untreated and terminal. With this metaphor in mind, I argue that the hegemonic discourse is inherently dangerous, and that it is deliberately used to divert, mislead, and deny in order to preserve the political-economic status quo.

That the monetary proceeds and the power are unequally distributed comes as no surprise; the problem of *why* people participate in their own disenfranchisement is what provoked Gramsci in the first place. To update the issues and apply them to the case at hand, what is it that makes an environmentalist plant a tree provided by big timber? Why does the public join organizations that create, promote, and defend such partnerships? How is it that we sanction the use of public funds and public lands to steer money into corporate hands, and respond approvingly when the government blesses the cooperation between industry, the planting groups, and "we, the people"? Before considering an answer, it is important to note that for hegemony to work it does not have to reach *all* of a society, it does not have to convince *everyone*. As a mechanism for preserving or strengthening the status quo, hegemony need only maintain the basic modes and norms of the community. Thus, even in a hegemonic society there is room for critics (though Gramsci spent the better part of his adult life in prison because of his views and potential influence). A hegemonic concept is powerful enough to derive strength even from those who consider themselves at odds with the power structure yet fail to challenge it in a fundamental way. Even tree planting, which is presented as a way to aid the world, may be complicit in the sustained degradation of the environment.

CELEBRITREES AND PLAIN OLD TREES

How is it that, in good conscience, we teach our children to care for nature while we continue to participate in its increasing degradation? In his book *The Giving Tree* (1964), Shel Silverstein depicts a relationship that has been taken as an apt parable for our interaction with nature and for the selfish and destructive behavior of our species. In the story, an apple tree generously and eagerly nurtures a boy who, as he grows through the stages of life, makes increasingly unsustainable demands that ultimately result in the destruction of the tree. Similarly, Dr. Seuss shows the perils of greed and the fragility of our environment in his book *The Lorax* (1972). Both of these books are considered environmental classics that, while ostensibly written for children, have been the subject of considerable attention in the adult world. Many of us were read such stories as children and have read them to our own children. We teach them to care, but what tools do we provide them with to effect change? What do we propose for a newly enlightened stewardship?

All over the country the answer is "plant trees." Millions of people have been members of the National Arbor Day Foundation, and many others have contributed to Global ReLeaf. Public service announcements from both groups reach tens of millions of Americans annually. They appear on the radio, on television, in the print media, as lead-ins to movies, on grocery bags, and in the curricula of our schools. Corporations such as Tommy Hilfiger and Eddie Bauer further spread the message by attaching it to opportunities to consume their products. Recognition of the value of trees is mandated as law and funded as public policy by the government, with dollars flowing from the legislature and expertise issuing from the Forest Service. And the timber industry is there to give us free trees, to sponsor our organizations, to provide us with the products we desire, and to assure us that this can all go on, under their stewardship, forever (see fig. 20).

Over and over again, trees are marshaled as a package of benefits and deployed across the American landscape. At times, we as individuals become directly involved in planting, though often it is our donations that permit organizations to get the trees into the ground. We participate in planting done by the government and the timber industry as consumers of their products, for they plant on our behalf. Given the list of benefits and all the wealth that we garner from these arboreal wonders, I have dubbed them celebritrees. Some are special to individuals because of a particular human affection (biggest, oldest, planted by me, provided shade for Elvis), but as a class, trees have no parallel in the natural world. Trees, according to the Forest Service, "are always working to help people"; is there anything else in nature that is simultaneously seen in such pervasively utilitarian and yet intimate and ennobling terms? Trees hold a cherished place on a human pedestal: they are arboreal heroes that will come to our rescue, now and in the future.

In order to challenge this particular discourse, the discourse of trees, it is important to remember that these celebritrees are also plain old trees,

Figure 20.   Even gullible idealists may smile—and wince—at their categorization by Tom Toles as a "renewable resource." Toles © 1998 The Buffalo News. Reprinted with permission of Universal Press Syndicate. All rights reserved.

or at least, some of them have that natural status. The tree planters' discourse harnesses the special regard that people have for trees and manipulates it for profit. For some, the profit is monetary, pure and simple. More complex is the "feel good" benefit that comes from planting trees. "Taking part" is a powerful concept. Taking part in caring for the environment by planting trees is enormously seductive. In this regard, the tree planting organizations serve as the stalking-horse of the capitalists, for they allow the public to engage in parasitic relationships with nature (which shows signs of growing crises), all the while believing they are changing the world for the better.

WHITHER THE TREES?

If people are inclined to focus on the symptoms rather than the causes of environmental degradation, the trees are not to blame. If we tend to enjoy our incorporation in the hegemonic mechanism and take pleasure in the trees we plant, that too may be "natural." But what now? After over a century of concern for the trees in the United States, and several millennia of rules and regulations to protect trees and the environment, what choices are we left with? I approach this question with trepidation, and will pursue it on two related levels. The first concerns the trees themselves and our interaction with the environment. The second concerns the broader hegemonic patterns and the character of our social systems.

Some two thousand years ago, the Talmudic sage Rabbi Yochanan ben Zakkai said, "If you should be standing with a sapling in your hand when the Messiah arrives, first finish planting the tree, then go and greet the Messiah."[16] His counsel remains good, and we should be planting trees, but not as a means to a messianic or Edenic world. If trees are to be linked to changing the world, perhaps in the future they can be planted as a monument to what we have accomplished, rather than as a badge of our often cheaply earned virtue. Rather than keeping a tally of what we have "saved," we should plant trees as a reminder of what we have wasted and what we must do to lessen our ill effect on the planet and on each other, so that there will be less need for remediation in the future.

If we are concerned about the environment, we must address the "associated power structures, social relations, institutional configuration, discourse, and belief systems" that contribute to its degradation.[17] For now, planting trees is not enough, and the partnerships we maintain with nonprofit groups, the government, and industrial America should signal the need for inquiry and concern, rather than serve as opportunities for self-congratulatory celebration. It is not that such relationships are bad by definition, but simply that the evidence shows that the condition of the environment is getting far worse, not better. Thus, those who point to their planting programs as the cure for environmental ill—that is, the government, the timber industry, and the planting groups—must be challenged to achieve their *stated* aims, at least the realistic ones, if they are to persist with such claims. And this involves changes that go far beyond the number of trees planted. Until they do so, their outreach to the public smacks of false advertising; these coalitions of power are a means, but their primary goal is profit rather than stewardship of the environment.

The world is too complex for me to have captured all the nuances of tree planting in these pages. In some places, of course, the local environment is improving, and some people are planting trees in ways that subvert the hegemonic conception. Ultimately, however, details are tools that help us to understand and verify the bigger pictures, thus I have focused on the discourse of tree planting and on the hegemony that draws upon, generates, disseminates, and benefits from it.

I have argued that trees are a particularly profound and powerful tool for reaching people and binding them to the status quo. Trees are part of our history, our culture, and in so many ways, our daily lives; their ubiquity lends itself—free of charge and innocent of complicity—to promulgation of the discourse of stewardship. This book is not solely about trees but also about power and the way it is constructed and wielded in our name and with our participation. Ostensibly the tree planters' hegemonic stewardship of the environment is carried out for our benefit and on behalf of nature. I do not think this is the case, and, at a more critical level, I believe that the structure of our society contributes to an arrogation, by capital interests, of the stewardship over many aspects of life in the United States and elsewhere.

Gramsci wanted to know why society failed to advance to a system that he believed would provide greater equality and social justice. His answer was that people are enticed into, and willing to submit to, a system that speaks of participation and representation if they can be led to believe they are truly stakeholders in the system of power and not just spectators. In 1972, a legal scholar asked if, in our society, "trees have [legal] standing"—that is, if they merit the power of self-representation in our system.[18] The answer to that question continues to evolve, but before it is answered, we must ask to what degree *people* have standing. In the current political and physical environment, it is essential to examine our standing as well as the standing of trees (and nature more broadly), and more important to challenge the power structures than to plant with them. Trees will survive human machinations on the planet, but in the meantime we must learn how to survive ourselves. Fundamental change will never come if we stand, sapling in hand, while the hegemonic powers continue to coast on their success at mollifying us. A reorganization of society and a reallocation of power—including a healthier set of relationships with nature—is out there. We must plant trees while we go out to greet them.

Notes

1. TAKING CONTROL OF NATURE

1. Michael Pollan, *Second Nature: A Gardener's Education* (New York: Atlantic Monthly Press, 1991), 202.

2. Throughout this book, I use the term *timber industry* as shorthand for the constellation of businesses supplying materials called by such names as "wood," "paper products," and "forest products."

3. I developed the theme of Eden in an earlier work, and my use of the term *man-made* is deliberate, in keeping with the gendering of nature and the predominance of men in the government, timber industry, nongovernmental organizations that focus on trees, and the history of environmental degradation. See Shaul Cohen, "Promoting Eden: Tree Planting as the Environmental Panacea," *Ecumene* 6, no. 4 (1996): 424–46.

4. Richard J. Moulton, "Tree Planting in the United States—1997," *Tree Planters' Notes* 49, no. 1 (1998): 10. Moulton reports a total of 1,623,978,000 trees produced by forest nurseries in the United States in 1997. Of that production, 3.3 percent came from federal nurseries, 21.4 percent from state nurseries, 52.5 percent from forest industry nurseries, and 22.5 percent from "other industry" nurseries.

5. Michael Williams, *Americans and Their Forests: A Historical Geography* (Cambridge: Cambridge University Press, 1992).

6. The realization that tree planting was both necessary and in the industry's interest did not occur overnight. A number of companies had greater foresight and phased out the cut-and-run orientation sooner than the rest. See R. Hidy et al., *Timber and Men: The Weyerhaeuser Story* (New York: Macmillan, 1963).

7. Michael Russo and Paul Fouts, "A Resource-Based Perspective on Corporate Environmental Performance and Profitability," *Academy of Management Journal* 40 (1997): 534–59.

8. *New York Times,* December 8, 1997, p. A17, emphasis in the original; and *American Forests* 103, no. 2 (summer 1997): 10.

9. Simon Schama, *Landscape and Memory* (New York: A. A. Knopf, 1996); Sir James Frazer, *The Golden Bough* (Garden City, N.Y.: Doubleday, 1978); Mircea Eliade, *Patterns in Comparative Religion* (Cleveland: World Publishing Company, 1970), in particular, chap. 8.

10. Eliade, *Patterns in Comparative Religion,* 265.

11. Robert Graves, *The White Goddess: A Historical Grammar of Poetic Myth* (1948; reprint, New York: Farrar, Straus, and Giroux, 1966).

12. Aldo Leopold, "The Forestry of the Prophets," *Journal of Forestry* 18, no. 4 (1920): 412–13.

13. John Perlin, *A Forest Journey: The Role of Wood in the Development of Civilization* (Cambridge: Harvard University Press, 1991); Schama, *Landscape and Memory;* J. V. Thirgood, *Man and the Mediterranean Forest: A History of Resource Depletion* (London: Academic Press, 1981).

14. Clarence J. Glacken, *Traces on the Rhodian Shore: Nature and Culture in Western Thought from Ancient Times to the End of the Eighteenth Century* (Berkeley: University of California Press, 1967).

15. Richard H. Grove, *Green Imperialism: Colonial Expansion, Tropical Island Edens and the Origins of Environmentalism, 1600–1860* (1995; reprint, Cambridge: Cambridge University Press, 1997), 25.

16. Ibid., 9.

17. John Evelyn, *Sylva, or a Discourse of Forest-Trees, and the Propagation of Timber in His Majesties [sic] Dominions* (1663; reprint, London: Scolar Press Limited, 1973).

18. Schama, *Landscape and Memory,* 168.

19. Research on the effect of trees in institutional settings consistently points to the benefit of being able to see trees. Violence drops in slum areas, patients recover more quickly in hospitals, and there is improvement in the condition of those struggling with mental health issues. See, among others, Robert S. Ulrich, "View through a Window May Influence Recovery from Surgery," *Science* 224, no. 7 (1984): 420–21; Kathleen Wolf, "Psycho-Social Dynamics of the Urban Forest in

Business Districts," in *People-Plant Interactions in Urban Areas: Proceedings of a Research and Education Symposium*, ed. P. Williams and J. Zajicek (Blacksburg, Va.: People-Plant Council, 1997).

20. Recent research has cast doubt on the utility of tree planting in regard to carbon sequestration. This is a complex issue, and I touch upon it in several of the following chapters.

21. International Paper, "Global Warming," *New York Times*, December 8, 1997, p. A17.

22. Dianne Rocheleau and Laurie Ross, "Trees as Tools, Trees as Text: Struggles over Resources in Zambrana-Chaucey, Dominican Republic," *Antipode* 27 (1995): 407.

23. Antonio Gramsci, *Selections from the Prison Notebooks*, trans. and ed. Quintin Hoare and Geoffrey Nowell Smith, 9th ed. (London: Lawrence and Wishart, 1971; reprint, New York: International Publishers, 1987). Originally published under the title *The Modern Prince and Other Essays*.

24. Dominic Strinati, *An Introduction to Theories of Popular Culture* (London and New York: Routledge, 1995), 168–69.

25. Timothy Luke, "Eco-Managerialism: Environmental Studies as a Power/ Knowledge Formation," in *Living with Nature: Environmental Politics as Cultural Discourse*, ed. Frank Fischer and Maarten A. Hajer (Oxford: Oxford University Press, 1999).

26. Michel Foucault, *The Archaeology of Knowledge and the Discourse on Language*, trans. A. M. Sheridan Smith (New York: Pantheon Books, 1972); Michel Foucault, *Power/Knowledge: Selected Interviews and Other Writings*, ed. Colin Gordon (New York: Pantheon Books, 1980).

27. David Demeritt, "Scientific Forest Conservation and the Statistical Picturing of Nature's Limits in the Progressive-Era United States," *Environment and Planning D: Society and Space* 19, no. 4 (2001): 431–59.

28. Eddie Bauer Corporation, *We're Not Out of the Woods Yet*, promotional pamphlet no. 7208 (Redmond, Wash.: Eddie Bauer Corporation, 1996).

29. Dr. Seuss, *The Lorax* (New York: Random House, 1971); Dr. Seuss, *The Lorax* (New York: BFA Educational Media, 1972), videotape.

30. Raymond Williams posits that *nature* is the most complex word in the English language. See, for instance, his essay "Ideas of Nature," in *Problems of Materialism and Culture*, ed. Raymond Williams (London: Verso, 1985), 67–85.

31. Roderick Nash, *Wilderness and the American Mind*, 3d ed. (New Haven: Yale University Press, 1982).

32. William Cronon, "The Trouble with Wilderness; or, Getting Back to the Wrong Nature," in *Uncommon Ground: Rethinking the Human Place in Nature*, ed. William Cronon (New York: W. W. Norton and Company, 1996), 88.

33. Carolyn Merchant, "Reinventing Eden: Western Culture as a Recovery

Narrative," in *Uncommon Ground: Rethinking the Human Place in Nature,* ed. William Cronon (New York: W. W. Norton and Company, 1996).

34. David Harvey, *Justice, Nature, and the Geography of Difference* (Cambridge: Blackwell Publishers, 1996), 119.

35. William Leiss, *The Domination of Nature* (New York: G. Braziller, 1972); Donald Worster, *Nature's Economy: A History of Ecological Ideas,* 2d ed. (Cambridge: Cambridge University Press, 1994); Donald Worster, *Rivers of Empire: Water, Aridity, and Growth in the American West* (New York: Pantheon Books, 1986); Karl August Wittfogel, *Oriental Despotism: A Comparative Study of Total Power* (New Haven: Yale University Press, 1957).

36. David Harvey, "The Environment of Justice," in *Living with Nature: Environmental Politics as Cultural Discourse,* ed. Frank Fischer and Maarten Hajer (Oxford: Oxford University Press, 1999), 163.

37. Eric Darier, "Foucault against Environmental Ethics," in *Discourses of the Environment,* ed. Eric Darier (Oxford: Blackwell, 1999), 234.

2. PLANTING PATRIOTISM, CULTIVATING INSTITUTIONS

1. George Perkins Marsh, *The Earth as Modified by Human Actions: A Last Revision of "Man and Nature"* (1863; reprint, New York: Charles Scribner's Sons, 1885).

2. William Cronon, *Changes in the Land: Indians, Colonists, and the Ecology of New England,* 12th ed. (New York: Hill and Wang, 1990); Douglas R. McManis, *European Impressions of the New England Coast, 1497–1620* (Chicago: University of Chicago, Department of Geography, 1972); Michael Williams, *Americans and Their Forests: A Historical Geography,* Studies in Environment and History (Cambridge: Cambridge University Press, 1992).

3. Cronon, *Changes in the Land,* chap. 8.

4. John Perlin, *A Forest Journey: The Role of Wood in the Development of Civilization* (Cambridge: Harvard University Press, 1991), chap. 12.

5. Williams, *Americans and Their Forests,* 17.

6. J. P. Kinney, *The Development of Forest Law in America: A Historical Presentation of the Successive Enactments, by the Legislatures of the Forty-Eight States of the American Union and the Federal Congress, Directed to the Conservation and Administration of Forest Resources* (New York: John Wiley and Sons, 1917), 179. This second piece of legislation was repealed four months later when the silk industry foundered as a result of low production and insufficient marketing.

7. Daryl Watson, "Shade and Ornamental Trees in the Nineteenth Century Northeastern United States" (Ph.D. diss., University of Illinois, 1978), 23–38.

8. Available at http://www.state.ct.us/emblems/tree.htm, December 14, 2002.

9. See Gayle Samuels, *Enduring Roots: Encounters with Trees, History, and the American Landscape* (New Brunswick: Rutgers University Press, 1999), chap. 2.

10. "Revolutionary War Symbol, the Liberty Tree, Is Cut Down," *New York Times,* October 26, 1999, p. A9.

11. Kinney, *The Development of Forest Law in America,* chap 2.

12. Increase Latham, *Report on the Disastrous Effects of the Destruction of Forest Trees Now Going On So Rapidly in the State of Wisconsin* (N.p.: Wisconsin Forestry Commission, 1867).

13. Richard Gordon Lillard, *The Great Forest* (New York: A. A. Knopf, 1947).

14. Andrew Jackson Downing, *Rural Essays: Horticulture — Landscape Gardening — Rural Architecture — Trees — Agriculture — Fruit, Etc., Etc.* (New York: R. Worthington, 1881), 304.

15. Ibid., 299.

16. Ibid., 301.

17. William Cronon, "In Search of Nature," in *Uncommon Ground: Rethinking the Human Place in Nature,* ed. William Cronon (New York: W. W. Norton and Company, 1996).

18. Downing, *Rural Essays,* 304.

19. Ibid., 309, 313. Downing was vitriolic in his condemnation of the use of exotic species and cast the use of native species as patriotic.

20. Government support for railroad tree planting came at the beginning of the twentieth century, when railroads were consuming nearly 1 million acres of timberland a year to support their operations, and concern was growing for their adequate supply. This support came in the form of funds supplied to the railroad companies so they could plant trees specifically for their own use. "Remunerative Tree Planting," *The Forester* 6, no. 3 (1900): 59.

21. Walter M. Kollmorgen, "The Woodsman's Assaults on the Domain of the Cattleman," *Annals of the Association of American Geographers* 59, no. 2 (1969): 219.

22. Ibid., citing E. Gale, "Forest Tree Culture," *Transactions* (Kansas State Horticultural Society; 1873): 13.

23. John Ise, *The United States Forest Policy* (New Haven: Yale University Press, 1920), 35.

24. 17 Stat. L. 605; Rev. Stat. of 1878, sec. 2464, March 3, 1873.

25. Kollmorgen, "The Woodsman's Assaults on the Domain of the Cattleman," 219; C. Barron McIntosh, "Use and Abuse of the Timber Culture [sic] Act," *Annals of the Association of American Geographers* 65, no. 3 (1975): 347–62. McIntosh cites Hitchcock from the *Congressional Globe,* 42d Cong., 2d sess., 1817–1872, pt. 5: 4464.

26. Kinney, *The Development of Forest Law in America,* 35.

27. Ise, *The United States Forest Policy*, 37.

28. R. Sassaman, "Early American Tree Planting: From Apple Seeds to Arbor Day," in *Helping Nature Heal: An Introduction to Environmental Restoration*, ed. R. Nilsen (Berkeley: Ten Speed Press, 1991).

29. Quoted in James Olsen, "Arbor Day: A Pioneer Expression of Concern for the Environment," *Nebraska History* (1971): 9.

30. Ibid., citing a letter to the *Omaha Daily Herald*, April 17, 1872.

31. Nathaniel H. Egleston, *Arbor Day: Its History and Observance* (Washington, D.C.: Department of Agriculture, Government Printing Office, 1896), 12.

32. Charles R. Skinner, *Arbor Day Manual: An Aid in Preparing Programs for Arbor Day Exercises* (Albany: Weed, Parsons, and Company, 1890), ii.

33. Ibid., 210.

34. Egleston, *Arbor Day*, 9.

35. Ibid., 17.

36. Ibid., 34.

37. Robert Schauffler, ed., *Arbor Day: Its History, Observance, Spirit, and Significance; with Practical Selections on Tree-Planting and Conservation, and a Nature Anthology* (New York: Moffat, Yard, and Company, 1909).

38. Ibid., 176.

39. On October 8, 1871, fire devastated the town of Peshtigo, Wisconsin. More than a thousand people died in the town and surrounding area, and the fire consumed more than a million acres of forest. Though forest fires were common, the magnitude of the Peshtigo fire could not be ignored.

40. John A. Warder, M.D., *Report on Forests and Forestry (at the Vienna International Exhibition, 1873)* (Washington, D.C.: Government Printing Office, 1875), 10, cited in Henry Edward Clepper, *Crusade for Conservation: The Centennial History of the American Forestry Association* (Washington, D.C.: American Forestry Association, 1975), 6. Clepper uses this quote to contest Gifford Pinchot's claim that he originated the term *conservation*, a claim made in his autobiography, *Breaking New Ground* (New York: Harcourt, Brace, and Company, 1947), 325.

41. Clepper describes in great detail the conservation aspects of American Forests in its first hundred years. That story is part of the broader literature of forests and conservation in the United States. See, among others, Henry Edward Clepper, *Professional Forestry in the United States* (Baltimore: Published for Resources for the Future by the Johns Hopkins Press, 1971); Ise, *The United States Forest Policy*; Kinney, *The Development of Forest Law in America*; Nancy Langston, *Forest Dreams, Forest Nightmares: The Paradox of Old Growth in the Inland West* (Seattle: University of Washington Press, 1995); Pinchot, *Breaking New Ground*; Andrew Denny Rodgers, *Bernhard Eduard Fernow: A Story of North American Forestry* (New York: Hafner Publishing, 1968); Henry Edward Clep-

per, *American Forestry: Six Decades of Growth* (Washington, D.C.: Society of American Foresters, 1960); Harold K. Steen, *The U.S. Forest Service: A History,* 3d ed. (Seattle: University of Washington Press, 1991); Harold K. Steen and Forest History Society, *Origins of the National Forests: A Centennial Symposium* (Durham, N.C.: Forest History Society, 1992); Gerald Williams, *The USDA Forest Service: The First Century,* FS 650 (Washington, D.C.: USDA Forest Service, 2000).

42. Details of the early years of American Forests and its various transformations are covered by Clepper in his organizational biography. As noted, there was an early merging of groups and several name changes along the way, reflecting the various agendas of the moment. The current name, American Forests, has been attacked by some group supporters for being grandiose, on the one hand, and so all-encompassing that it is meaningless, on the other.

43. "Announcement," *The Forester* 4, no. 1 (1898): 1.

44. Frederick Newell, *The Forester* 4, no. 1 (1898): 1.

45. B. R. Googins, "The Paper and Pulp Industry and Conservation," *American Forestry* 16, no. 7 (1910): 416.

46. National Lumber Manufacturers Association, "Forests and Parks— Forests and Play," *American Forests* 34, no. 10 (1928): 435.

47. Gifford Pinchot, "The Forester and the Lumberman," *Forestry and Irrigation* 9, no. 4 (1903): 177.

48. Herman H. Chapman, "Has the American Forestry Association Lost Its Former Usefulness? Reflections of a Director. Part 1: Policies," *Journal of Forestry* 19, no. 3 (1921): 285.

49. Ibid., 286.

50. Ibid., 290.

51. Ibid., 352.

52. Ibid., 347.

53. "What Is to Be Done?" *Journal of Forestry* 19, no. 3 (1921): 316.

54. T. S. Woolsey Jr., "After the Meeting of the A.F.A.—Ruminations of a Forester," *Journal of Forestry* 19, no. 3 (1921): 317.

55. Gifford Pinchot, *American Forests,* no. 4 (1929): 240.

56. Remo Lombardi, "They Planted a Million Trees: Boy Scouts of America Do Good Turn for Forests," *American Forests* (1929): 165.

57. Clara Bailey, "Farm Boys Plant Forests for the Future," *American Forests* (1939): 554.

58. Herbert Prescott, "New York's Great Planting Project," *American Forests* 11 (1929): 715; Stan Cohen, *The Tree Army: A Pictorial History of the Civilian Conservation Corps, 1933–1942* (Missoula: Pictorial Histories Publishing, 1980).

59. Clepper, *Crusade for Conservation,* 78–79.

3. THE NATIONAL ARBOR DAY FOUNDATION

1. John Rosenow, interview by author, Lincoln, Nebraska, October 16, 2000.

2. *Arbor Day* newsletter, special edition (n.d.): 4.

3. Membership figures are drawn from the circulation of the first newsletter of the fiscal year. Susan Erickson, director of member services at the National Arbor Day Foundation, provided these figures.

4. See William Cronon, "In Search of Nature," in *Uncommon Ground: Rethinking the Human Place in Nature,* ed. William Cronon (New York: W. W. Norton and Company, 1996).

5. *Arbor Day* newsletter (n.d.): 1–2. Emphasis in the original, as is the case for all of my citations of National Arbor Day Foundation material. Many of the foundation's materials are recirculated after some time, thus they often carry no identifying date or other number that would limit their future use.

6. Ibid., 2.

7. These images and the accompanying captions appear in the foundation's annual report for the year 2000 and many of its regular circulars as well. National Arbor Day Foundation, *National Arbor Day Foundation Annual Report, 1999–2000* (Lincoln, Nebr.: National Arbor Day Foundation, 2000).

8. *Conservation Trees* (Lincoln, Nebr.: National Arbor Day Foundation, n.d.), 4.

9. Membership survey (Lincoln, Nebr.: National Arbor Day Foundation, n.d.).

10. Membership letter (Lincoln, Nebr.: National Arbor Day Foundation, September–October 1998), 1.

11. Ibid.

12. Ibid., 2.

13. Membership letter (Lincoln, Nebr.: National Arbor Day Foundation, n.d.), 1.

14. *Arbor Day* newsletter, special edition (n.d.): 4.

15. National Arbor Day Foundation, available at http://www.arborday.org/trees/nineThings.html, September 6, 2002.

16. *Arbor Day* newsletter (May–June 1999): 6.

17. National Arbor Day Foundation, *National Arbor Day Foundation Annual Report, 1997–1998* (Lincoln, Nebr.: National Arbor Day Foundation, n.d.), 7.

18. *Arbor Day* newsletter (May–June 1999): 4.

19. National Arbor Day Foundation, available at http://www.arborday.org/trees/nineThings.html September 6, 2002, citing the work of Roger S. Ulrich, Texas A&M University.

20. National Arbor Day Foundation, 1998 Form 990, IRS Return of Organization Exempt from Income Tax. The Annual Report for 1998 lists grants allocated to specific National Arbor Day Foundation programs. They include grants from, among others, the U.S. Department of Education ($31,625), Department of Agri-

culture (totaling $203,627), Environmental Protection Agency ($127,600), and Department of Transportation ($12,084).

21. National Arbor Day Foundation, *National Arbor Day Foundation Annual Report, 1997–1998*, 9.

22. National Arbor Day Foundation, "Help Plant Trees across America," *All Hands* 960 (April 1997): 36–39.

23. The logic of including a pamphlet from the Poplar Council escapes me, though poplars are a favorite tree for biomass production.

24. Kevin Sanders, director of corporate relations, National Arbor Day Foundation, interview by author, Lincoln, Nebr., October 17, 2000.

25. These interviews, conducted with National Arbor Day Foundation staff at the headquarters in Lincoln and the Arbor Day Farm in Nebraska City, were open-ended and unstructured.

26. Two elements should be considered in relation to my interviews with the staff. First, the foundation sued a rival organization over exclusive use of the phrase *Arbor Day* and, in return, was savaged in court documents later quoted in the general press. Among the charges leveled were an array of personal and practical critiques of the way the foundation manages its affairs. I believe that fallout from this episode lingers, and that it makes the foundation skittish about inquiries. Second, the foundation staff is unaccustomed to probing by an academic and may have responded to my questioning in a way that exaggerates particular issues. On the whole, however, I think that representation of the National Arbor Day Foundation as an apolitical organization is important to the foundation's leadership, in both practical and philosophical terms.

27. Available at http://www.arborday.org/programs/RainForestRescue.html, September 6, 2002. In this quote the foundation refers to the greenhouse effect as "predicted"; elsewhere it is discussed without modifiers, i.e., as an unfolding process that is not disputed.

28. Mary Wickless, *The National Arbor Day Foundation Discovery Curriculum*, 2d ed. (Lincoln, Nebr.: National Arbor Day Foundation, 1996).

4. AMERICAN FORESTS

1. "Let's Plant Trees," *American Forests* 78, no. 8 (1972): 49.

2. Forest History Society, American Forestry Association Archives (FHS/AFAA), Box 85, Memo from Executive Director William Towell to American Forests Officers and Directors, "Tree Time U.S.A., a Project Proposal," November 29, 1972, 3. All internal American Forests documents cited in this chapter are housed at the Forest History Society in Durham, North Carolina, and are identified here with the abbreviation FHS/AFAA.

3. James B. Craig, "Accent on Incentives," *American Forests* 79, no. 1 (1973): 8.

4. FHS/AFAA, Box 75, Letter from American Forests Executive Vice President William Toll to Paul Ott Carruth, January 15, 1973, 1.

5. William E. Towell, "AFA's Call to Action: A National Tree Planting Conference," *American Forests* 78, no. 6 (June 1972): 4.

6. Ibid.; FHS/AFAA, Box 75, Letter from William Toll to Larry Painter, February 23, 1973, 1.

7. FHS/AFAA, Box 91, Memo from Board Member Richard Behan to American Forests Executive Committee, June 20, 1984, 3.

8. FHS/AFAA, Box 91, Letter from R. S. Wallinger to Perry Hagenstein, August 31, 1984.

9. FHS/AFAA, Box 91, Letter from R. S. Wallinger to American Forests Development Committee, June 11, 1984, 1.

10. FHS/AFAA, Box 91, Neil Sampson, "An Action Plan to Guide the American Forestry Association for the Calendar Year 1985," September 29, 1984, 9.

11. Ibid.

12. American Forests' executive director Neil Sampson wrote in defense of Burger King when it was targeted by the Rainforest Action Network for contributing to the deforestation of the Amazon. In a letter to the president of Burger King, he wrote, "I don't pretend to know anything about Burger King or your business operations, but if what you are doing is simply conducting business honestly in the market as it exists today, I'm on your side." FHS/AFAA, Box 91, Letter from Neil Sampson to Jeff Campbell, October 31, 1986.

13. FHS/AFAA, Box 91, "Content Analysis," Letter from R. W. Behan to American Forests Executive Committee, December 9, 1985, 2.

14. FHS/AFAA, Box 91, Letter from Neil Sampson to Perry Hagenstein, September 1, 1987, 1.

15. Ibid., 4.

16. FHS/AFAA, Box 91, Memo from Neil Sampson to American Forests Executive Committee, "National Legislative Initiatives," November 1, 1987, 2.

17. FHS/AFAA, Box 91, Memo from Scott Wallinger to Neil Sampson, August 18, 1988, 2, emphasis in the original.

18. Ibid., 1.

19. FHS/AFAA, Box 91, "ReLeaf for Global Warming," August 30, 1988, 1.

20. FHS/AFAA, Box 91, Letter from Perry Hagenstein to R. Scott Wallinger, September 7, 1988, 1.

21. FHS/AFAA, Box 91, Memo from Perry Hagenstein to American Forests Executive Committee, November 5, 1988, 1.

22. FHS/AFAA, Box 91, Letter from Lynn Day to Perry Hagenstein, May 5, 1989, 1.

23. FHS/AFAA, Box 91, Letter from Neil Sampson to Frank Paxton Jr., September 13, 1989, 1–2, emphasis in the original.

24. FHS/AFAA, Box 91, Memo from Scott Wallinger, "American Forests Mission/Policy versus Outreach—Legislative Goals," February 6, 1990, 1.

25. FHS/AFAA, Box 91, Memo from Neil Sampson to American Forests Executive Committee, "1989 Marketing, Membership, and Fundraising Plan," October 2, 1988, 2.

26. FHS/AFAA, Box 91, Letter from Mollie Beattie to Barbara Walker, November 30, 1989, 1.

27. FHS/AFAA, Box 91, Memo from Scott Wallinger to American Forests Board of Directors, October 14, 1988, 1.

28. *American Forests* 95, no. 11–12 (1989): 79.

29. American Forests, *Global ReLeaf, the Report* 1, no. 5 (winter 1989–1990): 1.

30. FHS/AFAA, Box 91, Letter from Neil Sampson to H. P. Newson, June 9, 1991, 2.

31. FHS/AFAA, Box 91, Letter from Perry Hagenstein to Charles Tarver, October 2, 1992.

32. FHS/AFAA, Box 91, Memo from Neil Sampson to American Forests Board of Directors, July 21, 1994, 2.

33. FHS/AFAA, Box 91, 1993 Progress Report, Neil Sampson, January 17, 1994, 15–25.

34. FHS/AFAA, Box 91, Global ReLeaf Strategic Planning Proposal, October 25, 1995, 5.

35. Deborah Gangloff, "Planting One for the Millennium," *American Forests* 102, no. 3 (1996): 13, emphasis added.

36. "Six Ways to Be Part of Global ReLeaf 2000," *American Forests* 102, no. 3 (1996).

37. *American Forests* 104, no. 2 (summer 1998): 10.

38. *American Forests* 104, no. 1 (spring 1998): 70 (inside back cover).

39. *American Forests* 107, no. 1 (spring 2001): 20.

40. American Forests membership letter, March 1998, 1, emphasis in the original.

41. Available at http://www.amfor.org/global_releaf/count_trees/count_trees_subhome.html, April 1, 2001.

42. Nancy Anne Dawe, "Everyone Loves Trees," *American Forests* 104, no. 2 (1998): 26.

43. Eddie Bauer Corporation, *We're Not Out of the Woods Yet*, promotional pamphlet no. 7208 (Redmond, Wash.: Eddie Bauer Corporation, 1996).

44. *American Forests* 104, no. 2 (summer 1998): 41, emphasis in the original.

45. American Forests membership letter, March 1998, 1, emphasis in the original.

46. Available at http://www.amfor.org/clmt_chg/carbcalc.php3, September 1, 2000.

47. Ibid. A later addition to the page, in small print at the bottom, reads, "American Forests' research in our Global ReLeaf sites shows that, on average, a tree removes .9175 tons of CO_2 during the first 40 years after planting. However, as trees grow, they compete for root space, sunlight, and water. Therefore, three trees must be planted to ensure that at least one makes it to 40 years." This type of information is very rarely provided by American Forests or any of the other tree promoters.

48. *American Forests* 107, no. 1 (spring 2001): n.p.

49. *American Forests* 103, no. 4 (autumn 1996): 29.

50. *American Forests* 103, no. 1 (winter–spring 1997): 41 (inside back cover).

51. *American Forests* 103, no. 4 (autumn 1996): 41 (inside back cover).

52. Ibid.

53. "Help Us Save Walden Woods," *American Forests* 103, no. 1 (winter–spring 1997): 38.

54. *American Forests* 104, no. 2 (summer 1998): 12.

55. Available at http://www.americanforests.org/planttrees/corporations, December 3, 2002.

56. Available at http://www.amfor.org/global_releaf/corporations/corps_why_work.html, April 1, 2001.

57. Ibid., 2.

58. Ibid.

59. "Corporations Go Green," *American Forests* 104, no. 1 (1998): 3.

60. Ibid.

61. Bob Leipold, "Healthy Planet: Good Business," *American Forests* 106, no. 3 (2000): 57.

62. Deborah Gangloff, American Forests, interview by author, Washington, D.C., October 23, 2000.

63. Urban Forestry and the Forest Policy are American Forests programs, which the organization referred to as "centers," subsumed since 1997 under the umbrella of Global ReLeaf 2000.

64. Champion International Corporation, "Forest Practices," *American Forests* 106, no. 3 (autumn 2000): 6. Champion International has since been purchased by International Paper.

65. Gangloff, interview by author, October 23, 2000.

66. The winner of the National Arbor Day Foundation's election was the oak, which received 101,146 votes, handily defeating the second-place redwood, which got 80,841 votes. All the other listed species received fewer than 50,000 votes each. My write-in ballot for dawn redwood (*Metasequoia glyptostroboides*) was lumped in the "other" category and did not carry the day.

67. Elvis Presley Tree is a registered trademark of Elvis Presley Enterprises. "Plant an Elvis Tree," *American Forests* 105, no. 4 (winter 2000): 6.

68. "Operation Silent Witness," *American Forests* 107, no. 1 (spring 2001).

69. "A Message from the Chair," *Annual Report of the National Urban and Community Forestry Advisory Council, 2002, p. 5*, available at http://www.treelink.org/nucfac/nf2002rpt.htm#letter, September 10, 2003.

5. UNCLE SAM PLANTS FOR YOU

1. Available at http://www.epa.gov/globalwarming/actions/national/difference/indopps/trees.html, p. 1, October 15, 1999, emphasis added. This page has subsequently become unavailable, but I have a copy of it in my possession. At the bottom of the Web page is the following notation about the site: "Presented by Eco-Tourist Journal and the Global Cooling TM Action Center."

2. Ibid., 2.

3. Available at http://www.epa.gov/globalwarming/actions/individual/difference/yard.html, September 17, 2002.

4. Richard J. Moulton and George Hernandez, "Tree Planting in the United States—1998," *Tree Planters' Notes* 49, no. 2 (2000). Planting statistics collected for the United States include numbers for Puerto Rico, American Samoa, the Commonwealth of the Northern Mariana Islands, the Federated States of Micronesia, Guam, and the Marshall Islands, in addition to the fifty states.

5. Available at http://www.fs.fed.us/pages/meetfs.html, April 20, 2001.

6. It would be easy to get sidetracked into explanations of the structure of the Forest Service and its evolution, but I will resist the temptation to do so. For information on the roots and development of the Forest Service, see, among others, Harold K. Steen, *The U.S. Forest Service: A History*, 3d ed. (Seattle: University of Washington Press, 1991); Harold K. Steen and Forest History Society, *Origins of the National Forests: A Centennial Symposium* (Durham: Forest History Society, 1992); Gerald Williams, *The USDA Forest Service: The First Century*, FS 650 (Washington, D.C.: USDA Forest Service, 2000); USDA Forest Service, *A Description of Forest Service Programs and Responsibilities* (Fort Collins, Colo.: USDA Forest Service and Rocky Mountain Forest and Range Experiment Station, 1989); USDA Forest Service, *Highlights in the History of Forest Conservation* (Washington, D.C.: USDA Forest Service, 1976).

7. Act of July 1, 1978 (P.L. 95–313, 92 Stat. 365 as amended; 16 U.S.C. 2101 [note], 2101–2114, 16 U.S.C. 1606).

8. "Cooperative Forestry," USDA Forest Service, available at http://www.fs.fed.us/cooperativeforestry, p. 1, April 20, 2001.

9. Ibid.

10. Available at http://www.r8web.com/spf/coop/default.htm, April 22, 2001.

11. Available at http://www.fs.fed.us/spf/coop/fip.htm, April 22, 2001.

12. Available at http://www.r8web.com/spf/coop/taxation/default.htm, April 22, 2001.

13. Available at http://ntsl.net/ntsl_mission.htm, April 22, 2001.

14. Available at http://www.fs.fed.us/cooperativeforestry, p. 1, September 18, 2002.

15. Act of July 1, 1978 (P.L. 95–313, 92 Stat. 365 as amended; 16 U.S.C. 2101 [note], 2101–2114, 16 U.S.C. 1606), sec. 9(a).

16. Available at http://www.na.fs.fed.us/spfo/pubs/urbanforestry/lab_ exercises/philosophy.htm, April 27, 2001, p. 1.

17. Available at http://www.fs.fed.us/spf/coop/ucf_general.htm, September 18, 2002.

18. Phillip Rodbell and Melissa Keeley, eds., *Urban and Community Forestry Accomplishments in 1999* (Newton Square, Penn.: USDA Forest Service Northeastern Area State and Private Forestry, 2000), 3.

19. "A Technical Guide to Urban and Community Forestry," available at http://www.na.fs/fed/us/spfo/pubs/urbanforestry/techguide/values.htm, p. 1, April 27, 2001.

20. The guide is produced by the Council of Tree and Landscape Appraisers and published by the International Society of Arboriculture, Champaign, Illinois.

21. "A Technical Guide to Urban and Community Forestry," available at http://www.na.fs/fed/us/spfo/pubs/urbanforestry/techguide/values.htm, p. 1, April 27, 2001.

22. Ibid.

23. Ibid.

24. Ibid., 2.

25. Thomas Green et al., *Illinois Small Community Tree Programs: Attitudes, Status, and Needs* (St. Paul, Minn.: USDA Forest Service, Northeastern Area State and Private Forestry, Urban Forestry Center for the Midwestern States, 1998). Available at http://www.na.fs.fed.us/spfo/pubs/urbanforestry/il_treesurvey/ frames.htm, April 28, 2001.

26. USDA Forest Service, *A Description of Forest Service Programs and Responsibilities*, 24.

27. Available at http://www.treelink.org/nucfac/nfback.htm, p. 1, September 18, 2002.

28. "A Message from the Chair," *Annual Report of the National Urban and Community Forestry Advisory Council, 1999*, available at http://www.treelink.org/ nucfac/nf99rpt.htm#_National_Urban_and, September 18, 2002.

29. From http://www.treelink.org/nucfac/nf99rpt.htm#_The_Challenge_Cost-Share, September 18, 2002.

30. National Association of State Foresters, available at http://www.state foresters.org/S&PF/U&CF.html, September 18, 2002.

31. Kevin McFarland, *Community Forestry and Urban Growth: A Toolbox for Incorporating Urban Forestry Elements into Community Plans* (Olympia: Washington Department of Natural Resources, 1994).

32. Ibid., 1.

33. Ibid., 3-4.

34. Ibid., 10.

35. Ibid., 12. There is no citation in the text for the Weyerhaeuser publication that mentions the Gallup Organization's study.

36. David Johnson et al., *Seeing the Forests for the Trees: An Oregon Urban Forestry Plan for More Livable Communities* (Salem: Oregon Urban and Community Forest Council, 1993).

37. Ibid., 7.

38. Ibid., 13.

39. Georgia Forestry Commission and the Georgia Urban Forest Council, *Georgia's Urban and Community Forest: An Assessment and Five Year Strategic Plan, 2000-2004* (Atlanta: Georgia Forestry Commission and the Georgia Urban Forest Council, 2000). Emphasis added.

40. Andy Lipkis and Kate Lipkis, *The Simple Act of Planting a Tree: Healing Your Neighborhood, Your City, and Your World* (Los Angeles: Jeremy B. Tarcher, 1990).

41. Ibid., xi.

42. Ibid., 1-2. Emphasis added.

43. Ibid., 2.

44. For examples of technical and forestry-driven books, see Arthur Plotnik, *The Urban Tree Book: An Uncommon Field Guide for City and Town* (New York: Three Rivers Press, 2000); Michael A. Weiner, *Plant a Tree: Choosing, Planting, and Maintaining This Precious Resource,* rev. ed., ed. Russ Weiner (New York: John Wiley Publishers, 1992). The jointly published book that I refer to is Jack Petit et al., *Building Greener Neighborhoods: Trees as Part of the Plan* (Washington, D.C.: American Forests and Home Builder Press, 1995).

45. Tony Secunda and John Goodchild, *Grow Your Own Trees: A Book and Seeds* (n.p.: Marlowe and Company, 1991).

46. Jean Giono, *The Man Who Planted Trees,* trans. Barbara Bray and Harry Brockway (London: Harvill, 1995); Dr. Seuss, *The Lorax* (BFA Educational Media, 1972), videotape; Shel Silverstein, *The Giving Tree* (New York: Harper and Row, 1964).

47. Eugene Tree Foundation, undated meeting announcement, copy in possession of the author.

48. Available at http://www.plantit2000.com/benefits.html, September 18, 2002.

49. Available at http://www.treesforlife.org/mothermag/mothermag.htm, May 9, 2001.

50. National Tree Trust, *Partner Handbook* (Washington, D.C.: National Tree Trust, n.d.), 1.3.

51. Ibid.

52. Ibid., 5.30. Since this list was composed, there have been some changes as a result of corporate consolidation; for the most part, however, the list remains the same.

53. National Tree Trust, *Planting America's Future: 1999 Annual Report* (Washington, D.C.: National Tree Trust, 2000), 20.

6. THE GREATEST GOOD

1. William B. Greeley, *Forests and Men: A Veteran Forest Leader Tells the Story of the Last Fifty Years of American Forestry* (Garden City, N.Y.: Doubleday and Company, 1951), 66. Greeley describes the phrase as Secretary of Agriculture James Wilson's "first commandment."

2. 16 U.S.C. 471, 499, 505, 568a, 569, 570.

3. S. T. Dana, "The Why of Forest Policy," *American Forests and Forest Life [American Forests]* 30, no. 364 (1924): 231. Cited in Henry Clepper, *Crusade for Conservation: The Centennial History of the American Forestry Association* (Washington, D.C.: American Forestry Association, 1975), 42.

4. Robert Gottlieb, *Environmentalism Unbound* (Boston: MIT Press, 2001), 13.

5. Harold K. Steen, *The U.S. Forest Service: A History*, 190.

6. Ibid., 195.

7. 16 U.S.C. 576–576b.

8. Alan J. Dominicci et al., *Forest Service's Reforestation Funding: Financial Sources, Uses, and Condition of the Knutson-Vandenberg Fund* (Washington, D.C.: U.S. General Accounting Office, 1996).

9. Forest Service Employees for Environmental Ethics, *Who Says Money Doesn't Grow on Trees* (Eugene, Ore.: Forest Service Employees for Environmental Ethics, 1998), 6.

10. The profitability of timber sales from national forest land has been called into question, but inasmuch as this is the premise of the Forest Service I use that language here. For a discussion of this controversy see, for instance, Jonathan Oppenheimer, *In the Red: National Forest Logging Continues to Lose Millions* (Washington, D.C.: Taxpayers for Common Sense, June 2001).

11. Richard J. Moulton and George Hernandez, "Tree Planting in the United States—1998," *Tree Planters' Notes* 49, no. 2 (2000): 5.

12. USDA Forest Service, *Reforestation and Timber Stand Improvement Report, National Summary Fiscal Year 1999*, report nos. 2400-D and 2400-M (Washington, D.C.: USDA Forest Service 2000), 5, 10. This figure includes 88,155 acres of "natural regeneration without site preparation"—i.e., after being cut, the site was left to be seeded by adjacent trees, which qualifies as "regeneration" under Forest Service terms.

13. Gerald Williams, *The USDA Forest Service: The First Century*, FS 650 (Washington, D.C.: USDA Forest Service, 2000), 127.

14. Available at http://www.fs.fed.us/land/fm/, June 1, 2001.

15. Williams, *The USDA Forest Service*, 149.

16. Maine Wood Products Association, "From Furniture to Fiddles" (n.p.: Maine Wood Products Association, n.d., mimeograph), collected October 14, 2000.

17. R. Hidy et al., *Timber and Men: The Weyerhaeuser Story* (New York: Macmillan, 1963), 505.

18. "Weyerhaeuser Sustained Yield Pays Off," *Weyerhaeuser News*, no. 47 (1961): 9.

19. Weyerhaeuser, "Harvesting Plans for the Next 100 Years," *American Forests* 52, no. 10 (October 1946): 482.

20. "Weyerhaeuser Advertising Builds Broader Image," *Weyerhaeuser News*, no. 58 (1964): 15.

21. Ibid.

22. Jean Mater, *Reinventing the Forest Industry* (Wilsonville, Ore.: GreenTree Press, 1997), 3.

23. Ibid., 44.

24. American Forest and Paper Association, *Sustainable Forestry Initiative Program Progress Report Overview, August 2000* (Washington, D.C.: American Forest and Paper Association), 1.

25. This was the membership as of June 2001.

26. American Forest and Paper Association, *Sustainable Forestry* (Washington, D.C.: American Forest and Paper Association, June 1995), 4.

27. Ibid., 14.

28. American Forests and Paper Association, *Principles and Implementation Guidelines* (Washington, D.C.: American Forests and Paper Association, 1995), 3.

29. American Forests and Paper Association, *Fifth Annual Progress Report, Sustainable Forestry Initiative Program* (Washington, D.C.: American Forest and Paper Association, 2000), 27.

30. Ibid.

31. American Forest and Paper Association, *A Tree for Each American* (Wash-

ington, D.C.: American Forest and Paper Association, n.d.), 10, copy in possession of the author.

32. Ibid., 1.

33. American Forest and Paper Association, "Healthy Forests for a Healthy Environment," in *Answers to Some Frequently Asked Questions about America's Forest Products Industry* (Washington, D.C.: American Forest and Paper Association, 1996), 1.

34. Ibid., 4.

35. John J. Garland, *Best Management Practices to Protect Water Quality* (Washington, D.C.: American Forest and Paper Association, 2000), 2.

36. The Yellow Ribbon Coalition, based in Springfield, Oregon, was a citizens group created to support timber-dependent communities through education and lobbying on forest issues during the political upheavals of the 1990s. Also on its wood products display was the slogan "From Pacific Northwest Families to Your Family."

37. *The Oregonian*, July 1, 1990, p. 8.

38. American Forests and Paper Association, *Principles and Implementation Guidelines*, 5.

39. Ibid.

40. American Forest and Paper Association, "Healthy Forests for a Healthy Environment," 11.

41. Available at http://www.internationalpaper.com/our_world/backupof-forest2_frame.html, June 1, 2001.

42. Boise Cascade Corporate Communications, *Boise Cascade and the Environment* (Boise, Idaho: Boise Cascade Corporation, 1995), 1; Boise Cascade Corporate Communications, *Boise Cascade . . . on Endangered Species Act Reform* (Boise, Idaho: Boise Cascade Corporation, June 1995). In the second brochure, Boise Cascade indicates that it supports the Endangered Species Act but believes it is "seriously flawed and has unnecessarily negative impacts on Boise Cascade and the entire country," and, therefore, calls for the Act to be reformed.

43. Weyerhaeuser pamphlet, n.d.

44. Weyerhaeuser, *The Concern for Biological Diversity* (Tacoma, Wash.: Weyerhaeuser, 1999), 3.

45. Ibid.

46. Boise Cascade Corporate Communications, *Boise Cascade . . . on Forest Management* (Boise, Idaho: Boise Cascade Corporation, June 1994).

47. Georgia-Pacific, *Growing Forests Forever* (Georgia-Pacific, n.d.). The contact person listed is H. P. Hornish; copy in possession of the author.

48. Available at http://www.plumcreek.com/environment/, June 1, 2001.

49. Available at http://www.internationalpaper.com/our_world/sf/increase .html, June 1, 2001.

50. Available at http://www.internationalpaper.com/our_world/millions_of_trees.html, June 1, 2001.

51. International Paper, "Global Warming," *New York Times*, December 8, 1997, p. A17, also available at http://www.internationalpaper.com/our_world/millions_of_trees.html, June 1, 2001.

52. Available at http://www.internationalpaper.com/our_world/millions_of_trees.html, June 1, 2001.

53. Available at http://www.internationalpaper.com/our_world/carbon_dioxide.html, June 1, 2001.

54. Available at http://www.simpson.com/environment.cfm?subject=forest, June 1, 2001.

55. John H. Rediske, "Forests Contribute to the Breath of Life," *Weyerhaeuser News* 9, no. 4 (1969): 7.

56. Ibid., 8.

57. Available at http://www.weyerhaeuser.com/ourproducts/timberlandsp/seedlingRequest.asp, June 1, 2001.

58. Http://www.unioncamp.com/corporate/environment/overview/forestry.html, November 1997, no longer available.

59. Donations from the timber industry to the 2000 presidential election campaigns revealed a clear and overwhelming preference for George W. Bush over Al Gore. Yet despite "pro-environment" Clinton administration policies, change in the management of federal lands had occurred at a pace that left the timber industry sufficient latitude so that the task of protecting the national forests remained, to a significant degree, with the courts. In the second Bush administration, there has been a clear tilt toward unfettered timber extraction, thus pressure on the forest, and the courts, has grown rapidly.

60. Derek Jumper, director of media, American Forest and Paper Association, interview by author, Washington, D.C., October 15, 2000.

7. CELEBRITREES

1. Michael Jaffe, "Paper and Forest Products," *Standard and Poor's* (New York: Standard and Poor's, 2000), 9. This is a rough estimate, with the figure for 1999 put at "more than $200 billion," which includes some revenue from nonforest and paper operations.

2. Ibid., 10. Weyerhaeuser owns or leases 38 million acres of softwood worldwide, and Willamette Industries had mills in the United States, Mexico, France, and Ireland.

3. International Paper, *2000 Annual Report* (Stamford, Conn.: International Paper, 2000), 38.

4. Exxon Mobil Corporation, "Planting the Future," *New York Times*, December 20, 2000, p. A31, emphasis in the original. The 13 million trees apparently refers to the company's work in Great Britain, though mention is made of many other activities to support tree planting in the United States and elsewhere.

5. International Paper, *2000 Annual Report*.

6. Robert Gottlieb, *Environmentalism Unbound* (Boston: MIT Press, 2001), 43.

7. Berhnard Schlamadinger and Timo Karjalainen, "Afforestation, Reforestation, and Deforestation (ARD) Activities," in *Land Use, Land-Use Change, and Forestry*, ed. Robert T. Watson et al. (Cambridge: Cambridge University Press and the Intergovernmental Panel on Climate Change, 2000), 173. See also S. Brown et al., "Mitigation of Forests for Greenhouse Gas Emissions," in *Climate Change — 1995 Impacts, Adaptations, and Mitigation of Climate Change: Scientific-Technical Analysis*, ed. Robert T. Watson et al. (Cambridge: Cambridge University Press for the Intergovernmental Panel on Climate Change, 1995), 775; and S. Gates, *Climate Change and Its Biological Consequences* (Sunderland, U.K.: Sinauer Associates, 1993), 249.

8. Royal Society, *The Role of Land Carbon Sinks in Mitigating Global Climate Change*, Policy Document 10/01 (London: Royal Society, July 2001).

9. Robert T. Watson et al., *Land Use, Land-Use Change, and Forestry* (Cambridge: Cambridge University Press and the Intergovernmental Panel on Climate Change, 2000), 4.

10. Ram Oren et al., "Soil Fertility Limits Carbon Sequestration by Forest Ecosystems in a CO_2-Enriched Atmosphere," *Nature* 411 (2001): 469–72. Also, William Lichter and John Schlesinger, "Limited Carbon Storage and Soil Litter of Experimental Forest Plots under Increased Atmospheric CO_2," *Nature* 411 (2001): 466–69.

11. For example, this sentiment was voiced by Deborah Gangloff, American Forests, interview by author, Washington, D.C., October 16, 2000; and Brad Williams, American Forest and Paper Association, interview by author, Washington, D.C., October 15, 2000.

12. Chris Maser, *The Redesigned Forest* (San Pedro, Calif.: R. and E. Miles, 1988).

13. Carolyn Merchant, "Reinventing Eden: Western Culture as a Recovery Narrative," in *Uncommon Ground: Rethinking the Human Place in Nature*, ed. William Cronon (New York: W. W. Norton and Company, 1996), 132–70; Mark Stoll, *Protestantism, Capitalism and Nature in America* (Albuquerque: University of New Mexico Press, 1997); Catherine L. Albanese, *Nature Religion in America: From the Algonkian Indians to the New Age* (Chicago: University of Chicago Press, 1990); Jennifer Price, *Flight Maps: Adventures with Nature in Modern America* (New York: Basic Books, 1999); Alexander Wilson, *The Culture of Nature: North American Landscape from Disney to the Exxon Valdez* (Cambridge, Mass.: Blackwell, 1992).

14. Evan Eisenberg, *The Ecology of Eden* (New York: Alfred A. Knopf, 1998), xx.

15. David Harvey, "The Environment of Justice," in *Living with Nature: Environmental Politics as Cultural Discourse*, ed. Frank Fischer and Maarten Hajer (Oxford: Oxford University Press, 1999), 161.

16. Mishna Rosh Hashanah 1:1.

17. David Harvey, *Justice, Nature, and the Geography of Difference* (Cambridge, Mass.: Blackwell Publishers, 1996), 184.

18. Christopher Stone, "Should Trees Have Standing? Toward Legal Rights for Natural Objects," *Southern California Law Review* 45 (1972): 450.

Bibliography

Albanese, Catherine. *Nature Religion in America: From the Algonkian Indians to the New Age*. Chicago: University of Chicago Press, 1990.

American Forest and Paper Association. *Fifth Annual Progress Report, Sustainable Forestry Initiative*. Washington, D.C.: American Forest and Paper Association, 2000.

———. "Healthy Forests for a Healthy Environment." In *Answers to Some Frequently Asked Questions about America's Forest Products Industry*. Washington, D.C.: American Forest and Paper Association, 1996.

———. *Principles and Implementation Guidelines*. Washington, D.C.: American Forest and Paper Association, 1995.

———. *Sustainable Forestry*. Washington, D.C.: American Forest and Paper Association, June 1995.

———. *Sustainable Forestry Initiative Program Progress Report Overview, August 2000*. Washington, D.C.: American Forest and Paper Association.

American Forests. *Global ReLeaf, the Report* 1, no. 5 (winter 1989–1990): 1.

"Announcement." *The Forester* 4, no. 1 (1898): 1.

Bailey, Clara. "Farm Boys Plant Forests for the Future." *American Forests* (1939): 554–57.

Boise Cascade Corporate Communications. *Boise Cascade and the Environment.* Boise, Idaho: Boise Cascade Corporation, 1995.

———. *Boise Cascade . . . on Endangered Species Act Reform.* Boise, Idaho: Boise Cascade Corporation, June 1995.

———. *Boise Cascade . . . on Forest Management.* Boise, Idaho: Boise Cascade Corporation, June 1994.

Brown, S., et al. "Mitigation of Forests for Greenhouse Gas Emissions." In *Climate Change— 1995 Impacts, Adaptations, and Mitigation of Climate Change: Scientific-Technical Analysis,* ed. Robert T. Watson et al. Cambridge: Cambridge University Press and the Intergovernmental Panel on Climate Change, 1995.

Champion International Corporation. "Forest Practices." *American Forests* 106, no. 3 (autumn 2000): 6.

Chapman, Herman H. "Has the American Forestry Association Lost Its Former Usefulness? Reflections of a Director. Part 1: Policies." *Journal of Forestry* 19, no. 3 (1921): 285–90.

———. "Has the American Forestry Association Lost Its Former Usefulness? Reflections of a Life Director. Part 3: The Secretary and the Finances." *Journal of Forestry* 19, no. 4 (1921): 327–53.

Clepper, Henry. *American Forestry: Six Decades of Growth.* Washington, D.C.: Society of American Foresters, 1960.

———. *Crusade for Conservation: The Centennial History of the American Forestry Association.* Washington, D.C.: American Forestry Association, 1975.

———. *Professional Forestry in the United States.* Baltimore: Published for Resources for the Future by the Johns Hopkins Press, 1971.

Cohen, Shaul. "Promoting Eden: Tree Planting as the Environmental Panacea." *Ecumene* 6, no. 4 (1999): 424–46.

Cohen, Stan. *The Tree Army: A Pictorial History of the Civilian Conservation Corps, 1933–1942.* Missoula: Pictorial Histories Publishing, 1980.

"Corporations Go Green." *American Forests* 104, no. 1 (1998): 3.

Craig, James. "Accent on Incentives." *American Forests* 79, no. 1 (1973): 8–9.

Cronon, William. *Changes in the Land: Indians, Colonists, and the Ecology of New England.* 12th ed. New York: Hill and Wang, 1990.

———. "In Search of Nature." In *Uncommon Ground: Rethinking the Human Place in Nature,* ed. William Cronon, 23–68. New York: W. W. Norton and Company, 1996.

———. "The Trouble with Wilderness; or, Getting Back to the Wrong Nature." In *Uncommon Ground: Rethinking the Human Place in Nature,* ed. William Cronon, 69–90. New York: W. W. Norton and Company, 1996.

Dana, S. T. "The Why of Forest Policy." *American Forests and Forest Life* 30, no. 364 (1924): 231.

Darier, Eric. "Foucault against Environmental Ethics." In *Discourses of the Environment,* ed. Eric Darier, 217–40. Oxford: Blackwell, 1999.

Dawe, Nancy. "Everyone Loves Trees." *American Forests* 104, no. 2 (1998): 26.

Demeritt, David. "Scientific Forest Conservation and the Statistical Picturing of Nature's Limits in the Progressive-Era United States." *Environment and Planning D: Society and Space* 19, no. 4 (2001): 431–59.

Dominicci, Alan, et al. *Forest Service's Reforestation Funding: Financial Sources, Uses, and Conditions of the Knutson-Vandenberg Fund.* Washington, D.C.: U.S. General Accounting Office, 1996.

Downing, Andrew. *Rural Essays: Horticulture — Landscape Gardening — Rural Architecture — Trees — Agriculture — Fruit, Etc., Etc.* New York: R. Worthington, 1881.

Eddie Bauer Corporation. *We're Not Out of the Woods Yet.* Promotional pamphlet no. 7208. Redmond, Wash.: Eddie Bauer Corporation, 1996.

Egleston, Nathaniel H. *Arbor Day: Its History and Observance.* Washington, D.C.: Department of Agriculture, Government Printing Office, 1896.

Eisenberg, Evan. *The Ecology of Eden.* New York: Alfred A. Knopf, 1998.

Eliade, Mircea. *Patterns in Comparative Religion.* Cleveland: World Publishing Company, 1970.

Evelyn, Sir John. *Sylva, or a Discourse on Forest-Trees, and the Propagation of Timber in His Majesties [sic] Dominions.* 1663. Reprint, London: Scolar Press Limited, 1973.

Forest Service Employees for Environmental Ethics. *Who Says Money Doesn't Grow on Trees.* Eugene, Ore.: Forest Service Employees for Environmental Ethics, 1998.

Foucault, Michel. *The Archaeology of Knowledge and the Discourse on Language.* Trans. A. M. Sheridan Smith. New York: Pantheon Books, 1972.

———. *Power/Knowledge: Selected Interviews and Other Writings.* Trans. Colin Gordon. Ed. Colin Gordon. New York: Pantheon Books, 1980.

Frazer, Sir James. *The Golden Bough.* Garden City, N.Y.: Doubleday, 1978.

Gangloff, Deborah. "Planting One for the Millennium." *American Forests* 102, no. 3 (1996): 13.

Garland, John. *Best Management Practices to Protect Water Quality.* Washington, D.C.: American Forest and Paper Association, 2000.

Gates, S. *Climate Change and Its Biological Consequences.* Sunderland, U.K.: Sinauer Associates, 1993.

Georgia Forestry Commission and the Georgia Urban Forest Council. *Georgia's Urban and Community Forestry Program: An Assessment and Five Year Strategic Plan, 2000–2004.* Atlanta: Georgia Forestry Commission and the Georgia Urban Forest Council, 2000.

Giono, Jean. *The Man Who Planted Trees.* Trans. Barbara Bray and Harry Brockway. London: Harvill, 1995.

Glacken, Clarence. *Traces on the Rhodian Shore: Nature and Culture in Western Thought from Ancient Times to the End of the Eighteenth Century.* Berkeley: University of California Press, 1967.

Googins, B. R. "The Paper and Pulp Industry and Conservation." *American Forestry* 16, no. 7 (1910): 415–18.

Gottlieb, Robert. *Environmentalism Unbound.* Boston: MIT Press, 2001.

Gramsci, Antonio. *Selections from the Prison Notebooks.* Trans. and ed. Quintin Hoare and Geoffrey Nowell Smith. 9th ed. London: Lawrence and Wishart, 1971. Reprint, New York: International Publishers, 1987.

Graves, Robert. *The White Goddess: A Historical Grammar of Poetic Myth.* New York: Farrar, Straus, and Giroux, 1966.

Greeley, William B. *Forests and Men: A Veteran Forest Leader Tells the Story of the Last Fifty Years of American Forestry.* Garden City, N.Y.: Doubleday and Company, 1951.

Green, Thomas, et al. *Illinois Small Community Tree Program: Attitudes, Status, and Needs.* St. Paul: USDA Forestry Service, Northeastern Area State and Private Forestry, Urban Forestry Center for the Midwestern States, 1998.

Grove, Richard. *Green Imperialism: Colonial Expansion, Tropical Island Edens, and the Origins of Environmentalism, 1600–1860.* 1995. Reprint, Cambridge: Cambridge University Press, 1997.

Harvey, David. "The Environment of Justice." In *Living with Nature: Environmental Politics as Cultural Discourse,* ed. Franck Fischer and Maarten Hajer, 153–85. Oxford: Oxford University Press, 1999.

———. *Justice, Nature, and the Geography of Difference.* Cambridge: Blackwell Publishers, 1996.

Hidy, R., et al. *Timber and Men: The Weyerhaeuser Story.* New York: Macmillan, 1963.

International Paper. "Global Warming." *New York Times,* December 8, 1997, p. A17.

———. *2000 Annual Report.* Stamford, Conn.: International Paper, 2000.

Ise, John. *The United States Forest Policy.* New Haven: Yale University Press, 1920.

Jaffe, Michael. "Paper and Forest Products." *Standard and Poor's.* New York: Standard and Poor's, 2000.

Johnson, David, et al. *Seeing the Forests for the Trees: An Oregon Urban Forestry Plan for More Livable Communities.* Salem: Oregon Urban and Community Forestry Council, 1993.

Kinney, J. P. *The Development of Forest Law in America: A Historical Presentation of the Successive Enactments, by the Legislatures of the Forty-Eight States of the*

American Union and the Federal Congress, Directed to the Conservation and Administration of Forest Resources. New York: John Wiley and Sons, 1917.

Kollmorgen, Walter. "The Woodsman's Assault on the Domain of the Cattleman." *Annals of the Association of American Geographers* 59, no. 2 (1969): 219–20.

Langston, Nancy. *Forest Dreams, Forest Nightmares: The Paradox of Old Growth in the Inland West.* Seattle: University of Washington Press, 1995.

Latham, Increase. *Report on the Disastrous Effects of the Destruction of Forest Trees Now Going On So Rapidly in the State of Wisconsin.* N.p.: Wisconsin Forestry Commission, 1867.

Leipold, Bob. "Healthy Planet: Good Business." *American Forests* 106, no. 3 (2000): 57–59.

Leiss, William. *The Domination of Nature.* New York: G. Braziller, 1972.

Leopold, Aldo. "The Forestry of the Prophets." *Journal of Forestry* 18, no. 4 (1920): 412–19.

"Let's Plant Trees." *American Forests* 78, no. 8 (1972): 48–51.

Lillard, Richard Gordon. *The Great Forest.* New York: A. A. Knopf, 1947.

Lipkis, Andy, and Kate Lipkis. *The Simple Act of Planting a Tree: Healing Your Neighborhood, Your City, and Your World.* Los Angeles: Jeremy B. Tarcher, 1990.

Lombardi, Remo. "They Planted a Million Trees: Boy Scouts of America Do Good Turn for Forests." *American Forests* (1929): 165–72.

Luke, Timothy. "Eco-Managerialism: Environmental Studies as a Power/Knowledge Formation." In *Living with Nature: Environmental Politics as Cultural Discourse,* ed. Frank Fischer and Maarten Hajer, 103–20. Oxford: Oxford University Press, 1999.

Marsh, George Perkins. *The Earth as Modified by Human Actions: A Last Revision of "Man and Nature."* 1863. Reprint, New York: Charles Scribner's Sons, 1885.

Maser, Chris. *The Redesigned Forest.* San Pedro, Calif.: R. and E. Miles, 1988.

Mater, Jean. *Reinventing the Forest Industry.* Wilsonville, Ore.: GreenTree Press, 1997.

McFarland, Kevin. *Community Forestry and Urban Growth: A Toolbox for Incorporating Urban Forestry Elements into Community Plans.* Olympia: Washington Department of Natural Resources, 1994.

McIntosh, C. Barron. "Use and Abuse of the Timber Culture [sic] Act." *Annals of the Association of American Geographers* 65, no. 3 (1975): 347–62.

McManis, Douglas. *European Impressions of the New England Coast, 1497–1620.* Chicago: University of Chicago, Department of Geography, 1972.

Merchant, Carolyn. "Reinventing Eden: Western Culture as a Recovery Narrative." In *Uncommon Ground: Rethinking the Human Place in Nature,* ed. William Cronon, 132–70. New York: W. W. Norton and Company, 1996.

Morgan, Robin N., and Kenneth Johnson. *An Introductory Guide to Urban and*

Community Forestry Programs: Urban and Community Forestry: Improving Our Quality of Life. Rev. ed. Forestry Report R8-FR 16. Atlanta: USDA Forest Service, Southern Region, 1993.

Moulton, Richard J. "Tree Planting in the United States—1997." *Tree Planters' Notes* 49, no. 1 (1998): 5–15.

Moulton, Richard J., and George Hernandez. "Tree Planting in the United States—1998." *Tree Planters' Notes* 49, no. 2 (2000): 23–36.

Nash, Roderick. *Wilderness and the American Mind.* 3d ed. New Haven: Yale University Press, 1982.

National Arbor Day Foundation. "Help Plant Trees across America." *All Hands* 960 (April 1997): 36–39.

National Lumber Manufacturers Association. "Forests and Parks—Forests and Play." *American Forests* 34, no. 10 (1928): 435.

National Tree Trust. *Partner Handbook.* Washington, D.C.: National Tree Trust, n.d.

———. *Planting America's Future: 1999 Annual Report.* Washington, D.C.: National Tree Trust, 2000.

Newell, Frederick. *The Forester* 4, no. 1 (1898): 1.

Olsen, James. "Arbor Day: A Pioneer Expression of Concern for the Environment." *Nebraska History* (1971).

"Operation Silent Witness," *American Forests* 107, no. 1 (spring 2001).

Oppenheimer, Jonathan. *In the Red: National Forest Logging Continues to Lose Millions.* Washington, D.C.: Taxpayers for Common Sense, June 2001.

Oren, Ram, et al. "Soil Fertility Limits Carbon Sequestration by Forest Ecosystems in a CO_2-Enriched Atmosphere." *Nature* 411 (2001): 469–72.

Perlin, John. *A Forest Journey: The Role of Wood in the Development of Civilization.* Cambridge: Harvard University Press, 1991.

Petit, Jack, et al. *Building Greener Neighborhoods: Trees as Part of the Plan.* Washington, D.C.: American Forests and Home Builder Press, 1995.

Pinchot, Gifford. *American Forests,* no. 4 (1929): 240.

———. *Breaking New Ground.* New York: Harcourt, Brace, and Company, 1947.

———. "The Forester and the Lumberman." *Forestry and Irrigation* 9, no. 4 (1903): 176–78.

Plotnik, Arthur. *The Urban Tree Book: An Uncommon Field Guide for City and Town.* New York: Three Rivers Press, 2000.

Pollan, Michael. *Second Nature: A Gardener's Education.* New York: Atlantic Monthly Press, 1991.

Prescott, Herbert. "New York's Great Planting Project." *American Forests* 11 (1929): 715.

Price, Jennifer. *Flight Maps: Adventures with Nature in Modern America.* New York: Basic Books, 1999.

Rediske, John. "Forests Contribute to the Breath of Life." *Weyerhaeuser News* 9,
    no. 4 (1969): 6–9.
"Remunerative Tree Planting." *The Forester* 6, no. 3 (1900): 59.
"Revolutionary War Symbol, the Liberty Tree, Is Cut Down." *New York Times*,
    October 26, 1999, p. A9.
Rocheleau, Dianne, and Laurie Ross. "Trees as Tools, Trees as Text: Struggles
    over Resources in Zambrana-Chaucey, Dominican Republic." *Antipode* 27
    (1995): 363–82.
Rodbell, Phillip, and Melissa Keeley, eds. *Urban and Community Forestry Accom-
    plishments in 1999.* Newton Square, Penn.: USDA Forest Service Northeastern
    Area State and Private Forestry, 2000.
Rodgers, Andrew Denny. *Bernhard Eduard Fernow: A Story of North American
    Forestry.* New York: Hafner Publishing, 1968.
Royal Society. *The Role of Land Carbon Sinks in Mitigating Global Climate Change.*
    Policy Document 10/01. London: Royal Society, July 2001.
Russo, Michael, and Paul Fouts. "A Resource-Based Perspective on Corporate
    Environmental Performance and Profitability." *Academy of Management Jour-
    nal* 40 (1997): 534–59.
Samuels, Gayle. *Enduring Roots: Encounters with Trees, History, and the American
    Landscape.* New Brunswick: Rutgers University Press, 1999.
Sassaman, R. "Early American Tree Planting: From Apple Seeds to Arbor Day."
    In *Helping Nature Heal: An Introduction to Environmental Restoration*, ed. R.
    Nilsen, 40–44. Berkeley: Ten Speed Press, 1991.
Schama, Simon. *Landscape and Memory.* New York: A. A. Knopf, 1996.
Schauffler, Robert, ed. *Arbor Day: Its History, Observance, Spirit, and Significance;
    with Practical Selections on Tree-Planting and Conservation, and a Nature Anthol-
    ogy.* New York: Moffat, Yard, and Company, 1909.
Schlamadinger, Berhnard, and Timo Karjalainen. "Afforestation, Reforestation,
    and Deforestation (ARD) Activities." In *Land Use, Land-Use Change, and
    Forestry*, ed. Robert T. Watson et al., 127–79. Cambridge: Cambridge Univer-
    sity Press and the Intergovernmental Panel on Climate Change, 2000.
Schlesinger, William, and John Lichter. "Limited Carbon Storage and Soil and
    Litter of Experimental Forest Plots under Increased Atmospheric CO_2."
    Nature 411 (2001): 466–69.
Secunda, Tony, and John Goodchild. *Grow Your Own Trees: A Book and Seeds.*
    N.p., Marlowe and Company, 1991.
Seuss, Dr. *The Lorax.* New York: Random House, 1971.
———. *The Lorax.* New York: BFA Educational Media, 1972. Videotape.
Silverstein, Shel. *The Giving Tree.* New York: Harper and Row, 1964.
Skinner, Charles. *Arbor Day Manual: An Aid in Preparing Programs for Arbor Day
    Exercises.* Albany: Weed, Parsons, and Company, 1890.

Steen, Harold K. *The U.S. Forest Service: A History.* 3d ed. Seattle: University of Washington Press, 1991.

Steen, Harold K., and Forest History Society. *Origins of the National Forests: A Centennial Symposium.* Durham, N.C.: Forest History Society, 1992.

Stoll, Mark. *Protestantism, Capitalism, and Nature in America.* Albuquerque: University of New Mexico Press, 1997.

Stone, Christopher. "Should Trees Have Standing? Toward Legal Rights for Natural Objects." *Southern California Law Review* 45 (1972): 450–57.

Strinati, Dominic. *An Introduction to Theories of Popular Culture.* London: Routledge, 1995.

Thirgood, J. V. *Man and the Mediterranean Forest: A History of Resource Depletion.* London: Academic Press, 1981.

Towell, William. "AFA's Call to Action: A National Tree Planting Conference." *American Forests* 78, no. 6 (June 1972): 4–5.

Ulrich, Robert. "View through a Window May Influence Recovery from Surgery." *Science* 224, no. 7 (1984): 420–21.

USDA Forest Service. *A Description of Forest Service Programs and Responsibilities.* Fort Collins, Colo.: USDA Forest Service Rocky Mountain Forest and Range Experiment Station, 1989.

———. *Highlights in the History of Forest Conservation.* Washington, D.C.: USDA Forest Service, 1976.

Watson, Daryl. "Shade and Ornamental Trees in the Nineteenth Century Northeastern United States." Ph.D. diss., University of Illinois, 1978.

Watson, Robert, et al. *Land Use, Land-Use Change, and Forestry.* Cambridge: Cambridge University Press and the Intergovernmental Panel on Climate Change, 2000.

Weiner, Michael. *Plant a Tree: Choosing, Planting, and Maintaining This Precious Resource.* Rev. ed., ed. Russ Weiner. New York: John Wiley Publishers, 1992.

Wesley, T. "After the Meeting of A.F.A.: Ruminations of a Forester." *Journal of Forestry* 19, no. 3 (1921): 317–18.

Weyerhaeuser. *The Concern for Biological Diversity.* Tacoma, Wash.: Weyerhaeuser, 1999.

———. "Harvesting Plans for the Next 100 Years." *American Forests* 52, no. 10 (October 1946): 482.

"Weyerhaeuser Advertising Builds Broader Image." *Weyerhaeuser News,* no. 58 (1964): 11–16.

"Weyerhaeuser Sustained Yield Pays Off." *Weyerhaeuser News,* no. 47 (1961): 9.

"What Is to Be Done?" *Journal of Forestry* 19, no. 3 (1921): 316–17.

Wickless, Mary. *The National Arbor Day Foundation Discovery Curriculum.* 2d ed. Lincoln, Nebr.: National Arbor Day Foundation, 1996.

Williams, Gerald. *The USDA Forest Service: The First Century.* FS 650. Washington, D.C.: USDA Forest Service, 2000.

Williams, Michael. *Americans and Their Forests: A Historical Geography* Cambridge: Cambridge University Press, 1992.

Williams, Raymond. "Ideas of Nature." In *Problems of Materialism and Culture,* ed. Raymond Williams. London: Verso, 1985.

Wilson, Alexander. *The Culture of Nature: North American Landscape from Disney to the* Exxon Valdez. Cambridge: Blackwell, 1992.

Wittfogel, Karl. *Oriental Despotism: A Comparative Study of Total Power.* New Haven: Yale University Press, 1957.

Wolf, Kathleen. "Psycho-Social Dynamics of the Urban Forest in Business Districts." In *People-Plant Interactions in Urban Areas: Proceedings of a Research and Education Symposium,* ed. P. Williams and J. Zajicek. Blacksburg, Va.: People-Plant Council, 1997.

Woolsey, T. S., Jr. "After the Meeting of the A.F.A.—Ruminations of a Forester." *Journal of Forestry* 19, no. 3 (1921): 317.

Worster, Donald. *Nature's Economy: A History of Ecological Ideas.* 2d ed. Cambridge: Cambridge University Press, 1994.

———. *Rivers of Empire: Water, Aridity, and the Growth of the American West.* New York: Pantheon Press, 1986.

Index

Page numbers appearing in *italics* denote illustrations.